Brain
Builders

Other books by Frank Minirth

Brain Builders

Easy Exercises
to Sharpen Your Mind

Frank Minirth, MD

SPIRE

© 2007 by Frank Minirth

Published by Revell
a division of Baker Publishing Group
P.O. Box 6287, Grand Rapids, MI 49516-6287
www.revellbooks.com

Spire edition published 2018
ISBN 978-0-8007-2907-3

Previously published in 2007 under the title *A Brilliant Mind* and in 2010 under
the title *Boost Your Brainpower*

Printed in the United States of America

Unless otherwise indicated, Scripture is taken from the New King James Version. Copyright © 1982 by Thomas Nelson, Inc. Used by permission. All rights reserved.

Scripture marked KJV is taken from the King James Version of the Bible.

Scripture marked NASB is taken from the New American Standard Bible®, Copyright © 1960, 1962, 1963, 1968, 1971, 1972, 1973, 1975, 1977, 1995 by The Lockman Foundation. Used by permission.

18   19   20   21   22   23   24   7   6   5

Contents

Introduction

S o you want a brilliant mind," I said with a twinkle in my eye to an inquiring seven-year-old. "Well, I can tell you how to develop one." She followed my advice, and she recently completed college with a 4.0 GPA, scored among the erudite on the MCAT, and will soon enter medical school.

Whether you are five or ninety-five, you can develop a more brilliant mind. Whether your IQ is 85 or 165, brilliance can be increased. Whether you are a child, a housewife, a blue-collar worker, or a business executive, brilliance is yours for the taking through the exercises contained in this book. The following pages will give you concrete tools to move in that direction. As surely as we can develop muscle cells with physical exercises, we can develop brain cells and connections with mental exercises.

Only 3,500 words separate the culturally literate from others. What words could you learn from religion, English, literature, art, music, math, physics, biology, and neurology that might elude many other people? The word lists in this book (containing over four thousand words and phrases) will help you close that cultural literacy gap and increase your mental power.

Each chapter begins with a quotation by a brilliant mind from science, literature, or the Bible. The passages are selected to illustrate how a better knowledge of words develops a brilliant mind.

Whatever your level of expertise—from a maven to a neophyte—you will benefit from this book. There are few who cannot learn from these simple techniques. On the other hand, there are few who will plumb the depths of the knowledge of this book. Whatever your age, a brilliant mind may well be within your grasp.

Oh, by the way, the young girl I mentioned earlier was my daughter, Renee. Just as she developed a brilliant mind, so can you.

1

A Brilliant Mind

A well-developed vocabulary is the outward sign of a well-developed mind. Words are the working tools of your brain, just as surely as your hands or your eyes.

Marilyn vos Savant
1946–

This is sage advice from the person with the highest IQ ever measured on the Stanford-Binet intelligence test. Normal is 100; Marilyn vos Savant registered 230. Another succinct admonition from vos Savant: "Every day, choose one word, one you're not sure you know, and look it up in the dictionary."[1]

Don't let anything stop you from increasing your memory power. Start with what you can grasp, and move from there.

I believe you'll surprise yourself with your brain's ability to stretch your memory beyond anything you thought possible.

●●●

Increasing brain power does not depend upon age, station in life, or intelligence; what matters is desire. No matter your age—seven, seventeen, fifty-seven, seventy-seven—you can exercise your mind. A desire to empower one's mental capacity, coupled with effective techniques of vocabulary recall, will lead almost anyone to excel. Thomas Edison, thought by many to have the highest IQ in the last millennium, was dismissed from school because his teacher thought he did not have the intelligence to succeed academically. Albert Einstein could not read until he was seven and still was considered a slow learner in high school. Winston Churchill was last in his class in school but developed a remarkable vocabulary that led him to become one of the greatest orators of all time. If Edison, why not you? If Einstein, why not you? If Churchill, why not you? Your mental muscles can be developed as surely as your physical muscles.

Most of us naturally use less than 5 percent of our overall brain potential. The development of the other 95 percent lies in our own hands. The brain can be tuned, developed, and improved. It is the most highly developed computer ever made, and yet the circuits and the cells must be sharpened until it becomes analogous to a highly tuned engine. By tuning your brain, you create innumerable new opportunities for growth, communication, and experience, and you save countless hours formerly spent retrieving information—hours that can now be spent in fruitful enterprise and relationships.

When I am on the radio, I respond to numerous questions ranging from biochemistry, physiology, and neurology to theology. Callers invariably ask me if I am using a computer to look up the information. I answer, "Yes, I have the most matchless computer ever made—the human brain."

You have that same potential; it merely awaits release. Good grades, job promotions, understanding in conversation, and the ability to persuade others—all are aided by the skills you can acquire from the tips and word lists in the following pages.

An Exceptional Tool

I have always loved words. Even in high school I enjoyed the study of words. The logic, I reasoned, was simple: we think in words; words are the tools of thoughts. With words we express our beliefs. With words we encourage others to act upon our beliefs. Others judge us by how we use words. Most standardized tests rely upon word identification in synonyms, antonyms, and analogies.

Different environments, people, and even opportunities to stand up for our beliefs and values all call for our ability to use words in a manner understandable to the subculture we are addressing. The right word allows us to connect with others. The French say that truth lies in nuances, and with the fine nuances of words we connect and communicate. Words are our showcase to the world. With words we create the perception we want to present. Indeed, words are of great price.

The average adult probably has a vocabulary of thirty to sixty thousand words. The highly literate may extend to one hundred thousand words. Yet the English language has well over one million words. Moving above the thirty-thousand-word range will greatly enhance our communication skills.

Why Memorize Words

Career success has been found to correlate with the number of words one knows. In the 1930s, Johnson O'Connor's famous research at the Human Engineering Laboratory of Boston on one hundred young men studying to be executives revealed that of those who tested in the upper 10 percent, all had executive positions five years later, yet none of those testing in the lower 25 percent did.[2] Many other tests since O'Connor's have confirmed the correlation between career success and vocabulary knowledge. For example, chief executive officers are consistently found to have higher vocabulary knowledge than any other group, even doctors and lawyers.[3]

We form concepts with words. Many standardized tests (GRE, MAT, SAT) involve vocabulary and language. Since neuroplasticity (more about this term later) does exist, we can increase IQ through words. As we learn words, the number of connections in the brain and the number of cells themselves increase.

In refining the following technique, I took a clue from the Chinese. Their language is extremely effective because it is simplified in many respects: no persons, no inflections, no tenses, no infinitives, no irregular verbs, and no articles; in short, simple though complex. The lesson I learned was to make the word definitions simple and short. The definitions are brief by design. The words are grouped according to related clusters: words describing other words, such as *large, small, good, food, speaking, agreeable, generosity, many, old, new, people*; words from different parts of speech, such as nouns, verbs, and adjectives; and words representing concepts, such as *experts*, *obedience*, *being careful*, and *wisdom*. I also encourage memory tips such as visualization with exaggeration.

The technique works, and why not? It is simple, is easy to use, is interesting, brings a diversion from worry, and promotes success in career or school. This tool is built on the concept of neuroplasticity, taking advantage of the fact that the brain can change in response to our experience—in this case, the experience of memorization.

How to Use This Book

The word lists contained in this book will start you on the road to increasing your brain capacity and even possibly forming new brain cells. Who wouldn't want that? Before we go further, however, a few comments are in order regarding how the word assignments were chosen. The brain can better comprehend a one-word definition than a long one. Thus, many of the definitions given are very short. Many words are also grouped for ease of learning—for example, nouns, verbs, adjectives, foreign words, similar words, prefixes, suffixes, word roots, and words from specific fields of cultural literacy (Christianity, English, literature, art, music, biology, neurology, and physics).

Finally, if the assignments seem numerous, remember that we are not seeking to cultivate an average mind but a brilliant mind. Don't let the number of words intimidate you. Begin with one assignment at a time and you'll be on the way to increasing your mental capacity.

Simply copy and carry one or two pages at a time in a handy pocket. And since we learn by spaced repetition, you must repeat the words on a word list several times daily until they are firmly fixed in your memory before moving to the next list. There are up to sixty words per word list to augment easy learning. The words in each section move from simple to difficult. They are intended to increase IQ scores, increase scores on standardized tests, and increase communication skills.

Incidentally, one of the tenets of memorization is review. Review of new words over a period of weeks helps to store the words in the permanent memory and adds to neuroplasticity. Because of the importance of review, some of the words are occasionally repeated in various lists.

2

Neuroplasticity

> I felt as if I were walking with destiny, and that all my past
> life had been a preparation for this hour and for this trial.
>
> Sir Winston Churchill
> 1874–1965

Winston Churchill evinced an unparalleled eloquence of the English language. He often chose, from his vast array of vocabulary words, rhetoric to stir the souls of his countrymen. With lucidity and a majestic style, he rallied England in a desperate hour during World War II with these words: "I have nothing to offer but blood, toil, tears, and sweat."

In 1953 Churchill was awarded the Nobel Prize for Literature for his mastery of historical and biographical presentation and his brilliant oratory.

Churchill's life also gives great credence to the concept of neuroplasticity. He was the lowest boy in the lowest class at Harrow School at age twelve. However, his love of the English language began to grow—it "got into my bones," he recounted. In 1895 Churchill graduated from the Royal Military College, and in 1940 he became the prime minister of Great Britain with a matchless command of words.[1]

●●●

Neuroplasticity is very popular these days, and it should be, for it may hold the key to brilliance for those who choose to exercise their brains as described in this book. *Neuroplasticity* simply means that the brain is capable of being molded: it can change and develop more connections between its many nerve cells so that, to a degree, it can even develop more cells. *Neurogenesis* is a similar term; it means that the brain is capable of growth and development.

This book can help you learn to develop your mind through the mental exercise of memorization. Memorizing words is not just a way to increase vocabulary, though that in itself is reason enough. In fact, memory exercises have been proven to actually cause neuroplasticity. Neuroplasticity offers you the opportunity to improve test scores, increase your IQ, memorize more information, communicate more effectively, be more productive at work—in other words, develop a brilliant mind. You can do more than just increase test scores; you can increase the capability of your brain. All of this is possible for you if you commit to exercise your mind with the lists of words contained in the following pages.

You can increase the number of synapses in your brain by memorizing words. The more words you memorize, the more you *can* memorize because of the increase in neural synapses. I know this to be true because I have learned it firsthand. I set out to test this by memorizing and reviewing a thousand words a day for a month. I was able to do so where I never could before, because I had been practicing the memory techniques and memorization lists such as the ones found in this book.

Before we begin the process of learning to increase our brain power, let's look further at the reality of neuroplasticity. Once you have grasped the principle of neuroplasticity, you'll be eager to move on to the mental exercises in this book so you can move from theoretical knowledge to experiential knowledge in developing a brilliant mind.

The concept of neuroplasticity was not an overnight scientific discovery. In fact, as early as the fifth century BC, Aristotle hinted at the concept of neuroplasticity when he said that we are what we repeatedly do.

Science began to pursue Aristotle's logic in the late nineteenth century when Ivan Pavlov (1849–1936) demonstrated that one could teach old dogs new tricks. In other words, through his famous canine experiment, he demonstrated that the brain could be changed or conditioned. Pavlov sounded a bell while presenting food to a dog, thereby stimulating the production of the dog's saliva. After the procedure was repeated several times, the dog would salivate with only the sound of the bell. Not long after, Edward Thorndike's (1874–1949) similar studies with cats and B. F. Skinner's (1904–1990) experiments with rats continued the investigation of the effects of reinforcement on behavior. These studies seemed also to demonstrate the nervous system's ability to change in response to experience.

In 1897 Charles Sherrington, a British neurophysiologist, coined the term *synapse* (the miniscule gap between two nerve cells) and stated that changes in neural connections were likely important for learning.

In the study mentioned in chapter 1, Johnson O'Connor of the Human Engineering Laboratory of Boston gave a vocabulary test to one hundred young men who were studying to become executives. The study implied that the top 10 percent of the test group—those who had executive positions five years later—had changed their nervous system by experience, and their greater facility to learn words increased their ability to think and to be successful.

In 1949 Donald O. Hebb, a psychologist, proposed that the functional relationship between a presynaptic and a postsynaptic neuron could change if excitation took place. (The presynaptic neuron sends the message over the synapse, and the message is received by the postsynaptic neuron.)

In the mid-twentieth century Wilder Penfield, a neurosurgeon, conducted research with thousands of people by stimulating specific brain regions while the subjects were conscious and aware of their surroundings. Stimulation could evoke clear and detailed recall of past events. Some memories were in words; others were visual. This again pointed in part toward the ability of the nervous system to change over time in response to experience.

In 1965 John C. Eccles, a 1963 Nobel Prize winner, proposed that learning and memory storage involved the growth of "bigger and better" synapses.

In the 1970s researchers used rats to demonstrate that the number of brain synapses increased when the test rats ran mazes.

In the 1990s research into neuroplasticity abounded. Studies revealed that adult mice living in "enriched" environments involving mental challenges produced additional cells in the brain's hippocampus. Also, researchers with monkeys and then with humans demonstrated that "enriched" environments increased brain cells. This indicated neuroplasticity. Furthermore, researchers proved that intellectual abilities are modifiable.

In addition, psychologist Julian Rotter's research showed how people who are motivated by "internals" (the feeling and resulting behavior that they could improve their intellectual abilities) did well in certain testing, while those who felt their intellectual abilities were determined by external factors did not do as well. In other words, those who tested higher were those who felt their intellectual abilities were pliable.

In studying thousands of students, psychology professor Carol Dweck found that they could be placed into two groups: one group believed that innate abilities are fixed; the other group believed that abilities such as IQ are modifiable. Consistently the group that believed their abilities were modifiable outperformed the group that believed their abilities were fixed.

In the early twenty-first century, researchers began to use PET scans to show that brain functioning is modifiable with behavior techniques. Their findings point toward neuroplasticity. Also, researchers using MRIs determined that only about 10 percent of variability in IQ is accounted for by brain size; there is considerable room for other factors to contribute to IQ. Sir Francis Galton (1822–1911), who invented the correlation coefficient, was wrong: head size does not significantly correlate with IQ. In addition, K. Warner Schaie, who investigated cognitive decline, found that the risk of cognitive decline could be reduced by three factors: higher education, extensive reading, and being married to a spouse with high cognitive status. All of this research continues to point toward neuroplasticity.

Finally, Bogdan Dragonski presented a study in *Nature* (2004) entitled "Neuroplasticity: Changes in Gray Matter Induced by Training." One group of participants was assigned to learn a complex juggling routine. The other group of participants had no such assignment. Each subject had a magnetic resonance imaging (MRI) at three points in the study: at the beginning, at three months, and at six months. On the second scan, the group of participants assigned the complex task demonstrated significantly increased gray matter in the brain's midtemporal area (which is involved in visual memory and mood) and in the left posterior intraparietal sulcus (which is involved in speech and motor movement). Though the increase dissipated on the third scan, in follow-up MRIs, the group that learned the complex routines still showed increased volume in the frontal and temporal lobes. In other words, the number of brain cells had been increased; the brain had neuroplasticity.

We've now seen how science has worked through the years to prove what used to be only theory. My contention is that a brilliant mind—indeed, a healthy, peaceful mind—may be within reach for many. Memory, and therefore IQ, has long been hypothesized to involve changes in the brain's neural circuits. Learning—one type of behavior—causes new synapses to form in the brain, and to a degree, these new synapses are responsible for IQ and a brilliant mind. Learning not only causes new synapses but to a degree also causes neurogenesis, the formation of new brain cells. You can indeed expand the capacity of your mind from the normal adult's 5 percent to a much higher percentage.

3

Memory Techniques

Genius is one percent inspiration and ninety-nine percent perspiration.

Thomas Alva Edison
1847–1931

Most scholars consider Thomas Edison to have possessed the highest IQ of the last thousand years. In light of that, his above statement should illuminate and encourage anyone who aspires to brilliance through the simple effort of learning new words. By the age of nine, Edison had read *The Penny Encyclopedia*, Sears's *History of the World*, Hume's *History of England*, and Gibbon's *Rome*. As he read, when he came across any difficult word or sentence, he would not simply pass it over, as many of us may tend to do, but would have his mother explain the word or phrase. This effort obviously increased his mental powers and led to the creation of a brilliant mind.

We too can aspire to brilliance by the diligent pursuit of learning words. Don't let anything stop you from increasing your memory power. Start with what you can grasp, and move from there. I believe you'll surprise yourself with your brain's ability to stretch your memory beyond anything you thought possible.

●●●

"How will I ever remember all of these words?" you may ponder. Below are eight time-proven memory tips that work for anyone. If vocabulary is the key to brilliance, then memory techniques turn the key. These tips definitely allow you to recall words, but they also render many other benefits, such as allowing you to recall names. A person's name is one of the most important words he or she hears. Remembering a name connotes a caring attitude. I've met people at my church who decided to return after their first visit because someone took the time to remember their name. A client who returned to my clinic after several years was astonished when I greeted him by name. This kind of memorization not only increases your mental capacity but also can bolster your relationships.

These memory techniques applied in another area can save you countless hours. Consider, for instance, how long it takes to look up a phone number. If you have such information stored at the ready in your God-given mental computer, you can fill your time with more important things. These techniques might help at work, for instance, by allowing you to recall valuable information at a board meeting. Indeed, these memory techniques have limitless application.

Eight Memory Techniques

1. Review

Many people can recall the meaning of a word if given the context but cannot give the meaning if asked outright. One key to memorizing new words is review, review, review—until the word moves from the periphery of your mind to your list of active vocabulary. Although this technique has been much maligned, it is the strongest with regard to word memorization, especially when combined with the other tips in this chapter. I suggest memorizing a set of twenty words and then reviewing that list daily for a week, and then periodically for a year.

Be sure to use your newly acquired words in conversation. This will help you retain them in long-term memory. For example, studies show that children retain 70 percent of what they say as opposed to 20 percent of what they hear.[1] Employ this technique of review in the other seven techniques for maximum effectiveness.

2. Employ Visualization

Memory comes from our five senses: vision, hearing, touch, taste, and smell. Of these, the strongest by far is vision. Children retain 10 percent of what they read, 20 percent of what they hear, but up to 50 percent of what they see.[2]

For example, when I learned the meaning of the word *meander*, I visualized in my mind "me and her" (my wife, Mary Alice) walking slowly (meandering) down a beautiful path. Create visual images for words, phrases, and names to increase mental capacity. Visualization is used in many of the following techniques.

3. Use Exaggeration

When I memorized the word *halcyon,* I visualized an old friend of mine, Hal, who was "calm" in the midst of a hurricane. This extension of visualization to even humorous extremes will help you remember. And the words will remain much longer in your memory bank.

4. Utilize Association

When I learned the meaning of the word *quintessence,* I visualized a boy approaching me, a boy who was in many ways the essence of his twin brother. *Quin* is associated in my mind with the sound of the word *twin,* and of course, twins are in *essence* many ways the same. Thus, I shall never forget that *quintessence* means the pure essence of something.

When I memorized the word *octogenarian,* I visualized a huge octopus with eighty arms. An octogenarian is a person in his or her eighties. Of course, an easier method here may be to simply use technique number 7 on page 27. *Octo* means eight.

The technique of association can be an invaluable tool in word memorization. Word analogies or associations are the basis of many tests. They are an exceptional learning tool. Many word lists for memorization in this book are grouped by association. They will fall into categories such as the following.

A. Similarities or Synonyms

small: infinitesimal

Associate the unfamiliar with the familiar. For instance, in the synonym above, visualize an "infant too small to see"—*infinitesimal.*

B. Contrast or Antonyms

gourmet: a person of refined taste

gourmand: a glutton

Both words begin with the letter g, yet they mean virtually the opposite of each other. To remember, visualize a gourmet "losing it" and becoming a gourmand. Actually, several associations are used in this example—sound, contrast, visualization, and exaggeration.

C. Subordination

butterfly—This is a familiar term.

chrysalis—This is an unfamiliar term. It refers to the undeveloped stage of a butterfly.

Visualize a friend, Chris, never growing up.

D. "Study of" Relationships

zoology: the study of animals

Other "study of" words are more difficult, such as hagiology, the study of saints. Visualize a hag who was miraculously changed and became a saint.

E. "Fear of" Words

claustrophobia: the fear of closed spaces

Other "fear of" words are more difficult, such as triskaidekaphobia—the fear of the number thirteen. Visualize this long word being fearful just as some people are afraid of the number thirteen.

F. "Type of" Associations

kangaroo: a type of marsupial

Visualize a kangaroo mired (or "marred") down in soup.

G. Working Tools

truncheon: a club of a policeman

Visualize the trunk of an elephant as a club.

H. Part to Whole

codicil: an added provision to a will

Visualize a clod who changed his will.

I. "Relating to" Associations

vernal: relating to spring

    Visualize that it is very near spring. True, this association is vague. (In fact, it may make more sense to someone who is from the South, because it recalls the Southern drawl.) But because this association is not vague to me, it becomes an astute observation. The association must make sense only to you.

By using associations with visualization and exaggeration, words can more easily be memorized. These are inimitable tools.

5. Use Classification

Many words are memorized according to the class or relationship they fall in. Hence, in this book there are lists with classes of words meaning small, big, bad, happy, rude, large, stubborn, angry, diligent, sad, expert, and good. Such words are overused until they are dull. The next time you are about to say "stubborn," try to summon another word. Try visualizing a stubborn mule: you cannot make tracks with him—he is "intractable"; he is a mule—downright "mulish"; he is more stubborn than any dog you have ever had—he is "dogged"; he will not cross to the other side of the road—he is beyond transient, he is "intransigent."

6. Command Yourself

You must concentrate to memorize, but concentration is not the whole process of word memorization; perhaps I should add the word *command*. When you direct the brain to do a task, it releases powerful chemicals in the direction requested. These chemicals are so powerful that if one hundred people with major medical depression—documented by a medical PET scan—are given a placebo, 33 percent will respond and their PET scan often returns to normal. They respond to the power of strong direction. Though they receive a placebo, they direct their brain toward recovery. Likewise, when you concentrate and then tell your brain to memorize something, potent chemicals are released to aid in the memorization.

7. Learn Prefixes, Suffixes, and Roots

Prefixes, suffixes, and roots are discussed elsewhere in this book, but no chapter on word memorization would be complete without a few comments on this most powerful technique. Since prefixes, suffixes, and roots hold the keys to thousands of words, memorize as many of them as possible. One prefix might hold the key to one hundred words. For example, *mal* means "bad." Thus, can you guess the meaning of *malabsorption, maladapted, maladjusted, maladministration, maladroit, malady, malaise, malapropos, malcontent, malediction, malefactor, malfeasance, malformation, malfunction, malignancy, malinger, malnourished, malpractice, maltreatment,* and *malversation*? Likewise, *pseudo* (false) is attached to almost a thousand words, so knowing one word helps in knowing a thousand more. The five hundred prefixes, suffixes, and roots in chapter 10 hold the meanings to well over ten thousand words.

8. See the Obvious in Foreign Words

Foreign words are discussed in chapter 12, but a few comments on how to memorize them are in order. Remember that much of the English language is derived from Spanish, French, German, and other languages. Thus, many of the spellings are similar. Consider the following words: *solitude* (English)—*solo* (Spanish); *debris* (English)—*debrie* (French); *October* (English)—*Oktober* (German).

A Photographic Memory

A photographic memory and a brilliant mind often go together. A photographic memory has traditionally been thought to be innate; however, if neuroplasticity is true, then a photographic memory can be developed. Incidentally, a photographic memory does not have to be 100 percent; anywhere from 5 percent to 95 percent will do.

A method of proof in math known as mathematical induction has application here. This method posits that if a statement is proved for one step in a process, the statement holds for the next step. By correlation and extension, brain synapses and cells can be developed through word memorization; so can a photographic memory to a degree. As you memorize the following words, labor on picturing the first few words of each list in your mind. Just as muscles can be developed, so can brain connections, cells, and photographic ability.

Summary

A good memory saves time, can catapult you to the top percentile on standardized tests, can create advancement in business, allows you to excel in a group, gives you the edge in negotiations, and can show evidence of your care when you remember another's name.

Vocabulary may be the key to success, but that key is worthless unless the words can be retained. In yesteryear, cultures such as the Greeks' originated memory techniques like those above, and generation after generation has added to them. These tips contribute to what we now call neuro-plasticity, the brain's ability to form new neural connections in response to new situations or changes in the environment.

As you make use of these eight memory tips, you will change your brain's environment and empower your mind's capacity to go way beyond a mere 5 percent.

4

Introductory Tests

"Therefore give to Your servant an understanding heart to judge Your people, that I may discern between good and evil. For who is able to judge this great people of Yours?" The speech pleased the Lord, that Solomon had asked this thing. Then God said to him: "Because you have asked this thing, and have not asked long life for yourself, nor have asked riches for yourself, nor have asked the life of your enemies, but have asked for yourself understanding to discern justice, behold, I have done according to your words; see, I have given you a wise and understanding heart, so that there has not been anyone like you before you, nor shall any like you arise after you. And I have also given you what you have not asked: both riches and honor, so that there shall not be anyone like you among the kings all your days."

1 Kings 3:9–13

Have you ever prayed for wisdom as Solomon did? Synonyms for the word *wise* include *astute, bright, brilliant, clearheaded, clever, commonsensical, discerning, insightful, intelligent, judicious, perceptive, perspicacious, prudent, rational, reasonable, sagacious, sapient, sensible, smart, sound,* and *understanding.* All of these terms point to gaining knowledge and increasing our mental capacity to apply that knowledge in all areas of life.

Just as Solomon asked for wisdom and received it, so can we. Incidentally, a prudent study of words wouldn't hurt our endeavor for wisdom. Exercising our God-given minds is crucial for gaining wisdom.

Research has shown that words should be memorized in order of increasing difficulty; this book is organized with that in mind. On the next page are some words to get you started. You'll find fifty in each memorization list. These test lists will help you determine your vocabulary level before you begin memorizing. In each introductory test, each list counts as one hundred points with each word counting as two points. Give yourself a grade for each of the following four tests.

If you score 50 to 74 percent on the following tests, you are in the superior range. If you score 75 percent or higher, you are exceptional—you have a brilliant mind. Whatever your score, you can move toward more brilliance as you memorize the lists in this book.

Introductory Test 1

1. abduct
2. brevity
3. charlatan
4. demur
5. eccentric

6. feasible
7. gourmand
8. hackneyed
9. immutable
10. judicious

11. kinetic

12. list

13. magnanimous

14. novice

15. obdurate

16. parsimony

17. quell

18. rancor

19. scrupulous

20. taciturn

21. unkempt

22. variegated

23. wrath

24. xanthic

25. willful

26. zealous

27. abridge

28. bequeath

29. capricious

30. daunt

31. effervescent

32. fallacious

33. garish

34. hardy

35. impecunious

36. jargon

37. kirk

38. lurid

39. meager

40. nuance

41. obscure

42. parochial

43. quiescent

44. replete

45. sage

46. temerity

47. unwarranted

48. vacillate

49. warlock

50. xenon

Grade _____

TEST 1 ANSWERS

1. to kidnap, 2. briefness, 3. a fraud, 4. to protest, 5. odd, 6. practical, 7. a glutton, 8. overused, 9. unchangeable, 10. wise, 11. lively, 12. to tilt, 13. noble, 14. a beginner, 15. stubborn, 16. stinginess, 17. to extinguish, 18. bitterness, 19. careful, 20. untalkative, 21. disheveled, 22. diversified, 23. anger, 24. yellowish, 25. headstrong, 26. fervent, 27. to shorten, 28. to give, 29. unpredictable, 30. to intimidate, 31. exuberant, 32. false, 33. gaudy, 34. robust, 35. poor, 36. professional language, 37. a church,

38. gruesome, 39. scanty, 40. a shade of difference, 41. vague, 42. provincial, 43. inactive, 44. full, 45. a wise person, 46. audacity, 47. unjustifiable, 48. to fluctuate, 49. a wizard, 50. a noble gas

----

Introductory Test 2

1. abate
2. bard
3. callow
4. demure
5. elusive
6. facile
7. guile
8. hiatus
9. idyllic
10. jubilant
11. kindle
12. lucid
13. marred
14. nefarious
15. obscure
16. protean
17. quixotic
18. rash
19. subtlety
20. tacit
21. usurp
22. vapid
23. wanton
24. xenophobia
25. yean
26. zealot
27. ascendancy
28. belated
29. credulity
30. deluge
31. egregious
32. florid
33. germane
34. hapless
35. ignominy
36. juxtapose
37. parvenu
38. labyrinth
39. medley
40. nullify
41. opulent
42. precipitate
43. querulous
44. rant

45. saccharine

46. tangential

47. utopia

48. vacuous

49. wistful

50. yahoo

Grade_____

TEST 2 ANSWERS

1. to decrease, 2. a poet, 3. immature, 4. reserved, 5. baffling, 6. easy, 7. deceit, 8. a gap, 9. blissful, 10. happy, 11. to inspire, 12. clear, 13. damaged, 14. evil, 15. unknown, 16. changeable, 17. idealistic, 18. hasty, 19. elusiveness, 20. unspoken, 21. to seize, 22. dull, 23. egregious, 24. a fear of strangers, 25. to give birth, 26. a fanatic, 27. dominance, 28. late, 29. gullibility, 30. a flood, 31. bad, 32. reddish, 33. pertinent, 34. unlucky, 35. shame, 36. to place side by side, 37. an upstart, 38. a maze, 39. a mixture, 40. to make void, 41. rich, 42. hasty, 43. complaining, 44. to rave, 45. sweet, 46. peripheral, 47. an ideal society, 48. stupid, 49. yearning, 50. a barbarian

---

Introductory Test 3

1. astute

2. benign

3. chagrin

4. deprecate

5. emulate

6. facetious

7. garrulous

8. halcyon

9. irate

10. jeopardize

11. kibosh

12. lassitude

13. maladroit

14. nonentity

15. obsequious

16. paltry

17. qualify

18. recalcitrant

19. sacrosanct

20. tenable

21. utilitarian

22. venerate

23. wag

24. xeno

25. Yahweh

26. zenith

27. accentuate

28. belie

29. chronicle

30. despot

31. extant

32. fabricate

33. genteel

34. heterogeneous

35. implore

36. justification

37. knot

38. lofty

39. melancholy

40. nocturnal

41. orator

42. prognosticate

43. quotidian

44. rudimentary

45. sordid

46. trivial

47. unprecedented

48. viable

49. wrest

50. yore

Grade _____

TEST 3 ANSWERS

1. keen, 2. mild, 3. humiliation, 4. to belittle, 5. to imitate, 6. humorous, 7. talkative, 8. peaceful, 9. angry, 10. to endanger, 11. to squelch, 12. weariness, 13. clumsy, 14. a nobody, 15. servile, 16. insignificant, 17. to modify, 18. defiant, 19. sacred, 20. defensible, 21. useful, 22. to revere, 23. a joker, 24. foreign, 25. God, 26. a high point, 27. to stress, 28. to give a false impression, 29. a record, 30. a tyrant, 31. in existence, 32. to invent, 33. refined, 34. mixed, 35. to beg, 36. a good reason, 37. a group of toads, 38. high, 39. sad, 40. occurring at night, 41. a public speaker, 42. to predict, 43. daily, 44. elementary, 45. dirty, 46. unimportant, 47. novel, 48. workable, 49. to turn, 50. time long past

---

Introductory Test 4

1. abhor

2. bauble

3. calumny

4. doleful

5. extol

6. fallacy

7. gambol

8. hacienda

9. incumbent
10. joust
11. kaput
12. lament
13. muted
14. nostalgia
15. oust
16. placid
17. quip
18. recant
19. savory
20. tangible
21. urbane
22. venial
23. wright
24. xylograph
25. yaw
26. zest
27. acclaim
28. battery
29. conundrum
30. dispassionate

31. emend
32. fortuitous
33. gambit
34. hone
35. inveigle
36. jaded
37. keen
38. levity
39. myriad
40. nebulous
41. onerous
42. ponderous
43. reciprocal
44. query
45. stanza
46. tentative
47. unbridled
48. vagary
49. wile
50. zephyr

Grade _____

TEST 4 ANSWERS

1. to hate, 2. a trinket, 3. slander, 4. sorrowful, 5. to praise, 6. a false assumption, 7. to skip, 8. a country estate, 9. required, 10. to fight, 11. broken, 12. to mourn, 13. silent, 14. homesickness, 15. to eject, 16. calm, 17. a joke, 18. to disavow, 19. tasty, 20. concrete, 21. polished, 22. forgivable 23. a worker, 24. a woodcut,

25. to turn, 26. a scraping of an orange, 27. to praise, 28. an assault, 29. a puzzle, 30. impartial, 31. to edit, 32. accidental, 33. a calculated move, 34. to sharpen, 35. to entice, 36. worn out, 37. a funeral song, 38. lightheartedness, 39. many, 40. vague, 41. burdensome, 42. massive, 43. mutual, 44. a question, 45. a division of a poem, 46. provisional, 47. unrestrained, 48. a whim, 49. a trick, 50. a gentle breeze

5

Parts-of-Speech Words

Mend your speech a little, lest you may mar your fortunes.

William Shakespeare
1564–1616

William Shakespeare is considered the greatest of writers in English. His literary masterpieces include *Romeo and Juliet*, *Hamlet*, *Macbeth*, *Antony and Cleopatra*, *The Taming of the Shrew*, *A Midsummer Night's Dream*, *The Merchant of Venice*, *Much Ado About Nothing*, *The Tempest*, and *Henry VIII*, to name a few.

Shakespeare sprinkled just the right words in just the right places to make a specific point, define a character, create drama, continue the plot, or provide a punch of comedy. Words such as *besieged*, *muting*, *yoke*, *munition*, *writhed*, *captivate*, *quillets*, *empress*, *forsworn*, *verbosity*, *abominable*, *frantic*, *wherefore*, *nunnery*, *divinity*, and countless more may not be used as frequently today, but they made Shakespeare's work come alive and stand the test of time. Like a master craftsman, Shakespeare used his knowledge of words to entertain audiences for almost five hundred years now.

● ● ●

The parts of speech serve as the foundation of literacy. Learning various words that are the building blocks of the English language is the starting point for your journey to a more brilliant mind. Therefore, we will start with various nouns, verbs, and adjectives. Begin your mental exercises with the following lists of up to sixty words.

I recommend that in all the following lists you put a check mark by words you do not initially know in each word section, then review all checked words until you know all the words in the list. Which words give you the most trouble?

Nouns

1. maverick: an independent person
2. elite: the best of a given group
3. amanuensis: a secretary
4. farrier: a blacksmith
5. internist: a doctor of internal medicine
6. lapidary: an expert in precious stones
7. extrovert: one who is outgoing
8. desperado: an outlaw
9. grandee: a nobleman
10. renegade: a traitor
11. thrall: a slave
12. malingerer: one who fakes illness
13. pettifogger: an unscrupulous lawyer
14. barrister: a lawyer

15. shamus: a private detective
16. proletariat: the working class
17. sycophant: a flatterer
18. bibliophile: a lover of books
19. miscreant: a villain
20. nabob: a bigwig
21. myrmidon: a faithful follower
22. thespian: an actor
23. bon vivant: one who enjoys food
24. parvenu: an upstart
25. vis-à-vis: one face-to-face with another
26. craven: a coward
27. braggadocio: a braggart
28. proxy: a substitute
29. votary: a person bound by vows
30. surrogate: a substitute
31. concierge: a doorkeeper
32. wayfarer: a traveler
33. gourmand: a glutton
34. demagogue: a corrupted leader
35. muckraker: one who exposes corruption
36. reactionary: an ultra-conservatist
37. waif: a homeless child
38. fob: a pocket watch
39. partisan: a supporter of a cause
40. calliope: a keyboard instrument at carnivals
41. coiffure: a hairdo
42. condiment: a seasoning for food
43. deluge: a flood
44. dossier: a bundle of papers with information
45. flotilla: a small fleet
46. cyclopean: massive
47. gorgon: a monster
48. rampike: a dead tree
49. reflex: unthinking behavior
50. ruse: a trick
51. victual: food

52. bibelot: an artifact
53. incubus: a nightmare
54. recreant: a coward
55. squib: a firecracker
56. guffaw: loud laughter
57. portmanteau: a bag for clothes
58. abbess: a nun
59. poltroon: a coward
60. cabochon: a precious stone

Nouns

1. knave: a deceitful boy
2. denizen: an inhabitant
3. enigma: a riddle
4. conundrum: a riddle
5. paradox: a contradictory statement
6. poser: a riddle
7. aficionado: a fan
8. apothegm: an adage
9. escarpment: a cliff
10. factotum: a handyman
11. sartor: a tailor
12. couturier: a tailor
13. courser: a spirited horse
14. adit: an entrance
15. allograph: a forgery
16. caudle: a drink for an ill person
17. canto: a division of a poem
18. malfeasance: misconduct
19. philomuse: a lover of poetry
20. imprimatur: a license to publish
21. regalia: the symbol of nobility
22. regent: a ruler
23. presidio: a military advance
24. jo: a sweetheart
25. din: a noise
26. diorama: an exhibit
27. fiat: an order
28. behest: an order
29. fob: a pocket watch

30. foray: a raid
31. gazetteer: a geographical dictionary
32. snafu: a complete foul-up
33. bonhomie: a friendly disposition
34. boon: a blessing
35. brouhaha: an uproar
36. acolyte: an assistant
37. guffaw: loud laughter
38. hoarfrost: frost
39. hologram: a three-dimensional image
40. hone: a tool for sharpening
41. interstice: a crevice
42. incursion: a raid
43. enclave: a small group
44. epaulet: an ornamental strip on a uniform
45. epigram: a pithy saying
46. epitaph: an inscription on a monument
47. epithet: a descriptive phrase
48. yen: a strong desire
49. epitome: a summary
50. apogee: the climax
51. erg: a unit of energy
52. noctambulist: a sleepwalker
53. legatee: an inheritor
54. munition: ammunition
55. incubus: a nightmare
56. melee: a free-for-all
57. meteor: a shooting star
58. nimbus: a halo
59. query: a question
60. shibboleth: a slogan

Nouns

1. yen: a strong desire
2. raconteur: a storyteller
3. brigand: a bandit
4. cant: meaningless talk
5. opprobrium: scorn

6. cornucopia: a symbol of plenty
7. nexus: a link
8. libertine: an immoral person
9. mendicant: a beggar
10. argot: a specialized vocabulary
11. interdict: an act of prohibition
12. interim: the time between periods
13. junta: a secret assembly
14. panegyric: a eulogy
15. ablution: a washing of the body
16. alcove: a covered recess
17. dossier: a bundle of papers with information
18. repast: a meal
19. condiment: a seasoning for food
20. confection: a candy
21. falsetto: an artificial high male voice
22. jingoism: extreme nationalism
23. lapidary: an expert in precious stones
24. lothario: a man who seduces women
25. métier: a vocation
26. odyssey: a long journey
27. paean: a song of praise
28. pettifogger: an unscrupulous lawyer
29. barrister: a lawyer
30. apothecary: a pharmacist
31. quid pro quo: something for something
32. rubric: an established rule
33. twerp: a silly person
34. waif: a stray
35. yahoo: a stupid person
36. yeoman: one who is loyal
37. amanuensis: a secretary

38. amicus curiae: a friend of the court
39. codicil: an addition to a will
40. coiffure: a hairdo
41. physiognomy: the external appearance only
42. satyr: a lewd person
43. skiff: a small boat
44. jetty: a projection into water
45. junk: a Chinese ship
46. ochlophobia: a fear of crowds
47. ophidiophobia: a fear of snakes
48. prevarication: a lie
49. rookery: a breeding place for birds
50. fifth columnist: a traitor
51. virago: an abusive woman
52. termagant: an abusive woman
53. ogress: an abusive woman
54. harpy: an abusive woman
55. theodicy: divine justice
56. teleology: the doctrine that final cause exists
57. syllogism: a false reasoning
58. eschatology: the study of last things
59. votary: a person bound by vows
60. threnody: a funeral song

Nouns

1. palmetto: a palm tree
2. epoch: a noteworthy period
3. mien: the external appearance
4. miscreant: a villain
5. nostrum: a quack remedy
6. surcharge: an additional tax

7. cataract: a dullness of the eye

8. functionary: an official

9. obelisk: a tapering column

10. voussoir: a wedge-shaped stone

11. edifice: a monument

12. bastille: a fortification

13. bastion: a fortification

14. bulwark: a defensive wall

15. corrigendum: an error

16. erratum: an error

17. cartographer: a mapmaker

18. chutzpah: audacity

19. hubris: audacity

20. cryogenics: the science of freezing

21. respite: a rest

22. sodality: a club

23. xenophobia: a fear of strangers

24. plebiscite: a direct vote

25. ogre: a wicked person

26. ordnance: military supplies

27. plaintiff: a person who brings a complaint

28. pratfall: a failure or fall

29. pundit: an expert

30. gaffe: a mistake

31. faux pas: a mistake

32. gremlin: a bad influence

33. hagiography: a biography of a saint

34. horology: the science of measuring time

35. conveyance: a deed

36. cardigan: an open-front sweater

37. atoll: a coral island

38. veranda: an open porch

39. dinghy: a boat

40. surety: a guarantee

41. caisson: an ammunition vehicle

42. aquifer: a water-bearing rock

43. gantry: a movable structure

44. moraine: a glacial deposit

45. botanicals: herbs
46. tofu: a soybean product
47. squib: a short news item
48. grist: a grain
49. nee: birth name
50. lee: a shelter
51. cloche: a glass cover
52. napery: a linen
53. serape: a woolen blanket
54. dais: a platform
55. précis: a summary
56. dam: an animal's mother
57. prig: a self-righteous person
58. chaff: grain husks
59. clutch: a group of eggs
60. conch: a shell

Nouns

1. deputation: a delegation
2. lagniappe: a small gift
3. vespers: evening church services
4. portico: a porch
5. abnegation: a denial
6. artifice: deception
7. carnage: a slaughter
8. consort: a companion
9. conclave: a closed meeting
10. depredation: a plundering
11. dint: a blow
12. epilogue: a closing section of a novel
13. epigraph: an inscription on a statue
14. fealty: loyalty
15. magnate: an influential person
16. nemesis: one that inflicts vengeance
17. nexus: a connection
18. obloquy: verbal abuse
19. perdition: complete loss

20. pommel: the front of a saddle
21. protocol: an original record
22. shoal: a great quantity
23. tether: a rope
24. throes: anguish
25. troth: belief
26. vagary: an eccentric idea
27. vertigo: dizziness
28. vicissitude: a change of circumstances
29. codicil: an addition to a will
30. annex: an addition to a section of a building
31. proviso: an addition to a document
32. tumbrel: a cart
33. onus: a burden
34. mote: a tiny piece of dust
35. stripling: an adolescent
36. gadfly: an annoyance
37. jamb: a vertical support
38. girder: a horizontal support
39. buss: a kiss
40. compeer: a peer
41. reliquary: a structure that holds artifacts
42. terrarium: a structure that holds plants
43. meniscus: the top surface of a liquid
44. fray: a fight
45. spoof: a joke
46. clerestory: a wall
47. punctilio: a fine point of etiquette
48. quisling: one who betrays
49. bailiwick: one's area of skill
50. prefect: a government official
51. gastronomy: the study of good eating
52. patronymics: surnames or last names
53. badinage: teasing talk
54. cynosure: the center of attention

55. farrago: a mixture
56. oscitancy: drowsiness
57. osculation: the act of kissing
58. rung: a step of a ladder
59. yelp: a short bark
60. chantey: a song for the sea

Nouns

1. slalom: ski racing
2. hart: a male deer
3. dither: a fit of indecision
4. anode: a positively charged electrode
5. cathode: a negatively charged electrode
6. spar: a horizontal support
7. espalier: a horizontal support
8. protocol: the rules of behavior
9. habiliment: the rules of dress
10. olio: a mixture
11. colophon: the final section of a book
12. coda: the final passage in a music movement
13. mollycoddle: a sissy
14. harridan: a hag
15. dirigible: an airship
16. nosology: the classification of diseases
17. rill: a stream
18. cassock: the clothing worn by a priest
19. wimple: the clothing worn by a nun
20. escarpment: a hill
21. fourth estate: the media
22. fifth columnist: a traitor
23. barbican: a fortification
24. egress: an exit
25. exchequer: a national treasury
26. pang: a pain

27. stanza: a subsection of a poem
28. ague: malarial fever
29. archipelago: a group of islands
30. boon: a benefit
31. anthology: a collection of writings
32. lineage: ancestry

Verbs

1. hobnob: to associate
2. deign: to condescend
3. quail: to lose courage
4. decimate: to destroy
5. exhume: to unearth
6. purloin: to steal
7. eke: to earn with difficulty
8. mete: to allot
9. immolate: to kill
10. incarcerate: to jail
11. abscond: to escape the law
12. roister: to boast
13. beguile: to charm
14. assuage: to lessen
15. gainsay: to deny
16. qui vive: to be on the alert
17. bilk: to deceive
18. addle: to muddle
19. careen: to cause to lean
20. abominate: to hate
21. raze: to tear down completely
22. abstain: to deny oneself
23. placate: to soothe
24. accede: to yield
25. rebuff: to reject
26. wane: to decrease
27. accentuate: to emphasize
28. nurture: to nourish
29. obfuscate: to obscure
30. obliterate: to destroy
31. undermine: to damage
32. relegate: to shift to an inferior position

33. obtrude: to impose oneself on others
34. rout: to defeat
35. repudiate: to reject
36. expedite: to speed up
37. scorn: to treat with disrespect
38. hamper: to impede
39. emulate: to imitate
40. emanate: to emit
41. solicit: to ask for
42. vivify: to quicken
43. extricate: to free from entanglement
44. oust: to force out
45. rescind: to cancel
46. pacify: to appease
47. squander: to waste
48. palliate: to mitigate
49. veer: to change in direction
50. truckle: to yield to a superior
51. transcribe: to record
52. transcend: to rise above
53. palpitate: to pulsate
54. pan: to censure
55. parry: to ward off a blow
56. patronize: to treat as inferior
57. cleave: to adhere to
58. coddle: to pamper
59. complement: to complete
60. concede: to admit

Verbs

1. mitigate: to make less severe
2. abate: to reduce
3. abash: to embarrass
4. abet: to aid
5. abhor: to hate
6. garner: to collect
7. obliterate: to erase
8. abide: to remain
9. nullify: to negate
10. aver: to state
11. mar: to damage

12. writhe: to twist
13. wrest: to take by violence
14. heed: to consider
15. winnow: to rid of undesirable parts
16. meander: to wander casually
17. abnegate: to deny oneself
18. obscure: to make unclear
19. abrogate: to abolish
20. peruse: to study
21. abjure: to renounce
22. adjure: to beg
23. adulterate: to corrupt
24. arrogate: to demand
25. batten: to thrive
26. besmirch: to soil
27. broach: to introduce
28. cavil: to find fault
29. chafe: to fret
30. comport: to agree
31. contravene: to oppose
32. decry: to condemn
33. descry: to catch sight of
34. descant: to comment at length
35. despoil: to rob
36. egress: to depart
37. elucidate: to explain
38. endue: to provide
39. eschew: to avoid
40. expunge: to delete
41. feign: to pretend
42. ferment: to excite
43. foist: to impose
44. galvanize: to excite
45. imprecate: to pray for evil
46. indemnity: to protect against loss
47. lacerate: to tear
48. obfuscate: to confuse
49. obtrude: to eject
50. preponderate: to outweigh
51. propagate: to reproduce
52. purloin: to steal
53. reprehend: to reprimand
54. scourge: to whip

55. stanch: to stop the flow of blood
56. supplant: to replace
57. surfeit: to supply in excess
58. swathe: to wrap
59. traduce: to slander
60. vouchsafe: to grant

Verbs

1. accede: to agree
2. assent: to agree
3. concur: to agree
4. assert: to state
5. affirm: to state
6. avow: to state
7. asseverate: to state
8. hamper: to hinder
9. importune: to trouble
10. succor: to help
11. obviate: to prevent
12. supplicate: to beg
13. beseech: to beg
14. capitulate: to yield
15. recapitulate: to summarize
16. truncate: to shorten
17. abridge: to shorten
18. curtail: to shorten
19. enervate: to weaken
20. gentrify: to upgrade
21. mortify: to humiliate
22. procure: to obtain
23. kibitz: to give unwanted advice
24. ferret: to search
25. ransack: to search
26. vitiate: to make worthless
27. meld: to merge
28. cosset: to coddle
29. quail: to lose courage
30. preen: to dress up
31. cobble: to make hastily
32. roil: to make angry
33. sear: to scorch
34. abjure: to reject
35. interpolate: to insert

36. extrapolate: to estimate
37. immolate: to kill
38. course: to flow
39. brook: to tolerate
40. yaw: to change directions
41. deracinate: to uproot
42. cashier: to dismiss
43. peculate: to steal
44. vitiate: to ruin
45. malinger: to feign illness
46. descant: to elaborate
47. excoriate: to rebuke
48. traduce: to disgrace
49. extirpate: to destroy
50. cachinnate: to laugh
51. manumit: to free
52. fulminate: to explode
53. scarify: to distress
54. expatriate: to banish
55. surmount: to surpass
56. cuff: to hit
57. skewer: to pierce
58. collar: to seize
59. troll: to fish
60. beard: to confront

Verbs

1. divagate: to wander
2. surmount: to surpass
3. survey: to examine
4. prance: to caper
5. gull: to trick
6. cuff: to hit
7. fray: to tatter
8. carp: to complain
9. vend: to hawk
10. hawk: to peddle
11. rig: to outfit
12. cobble: to mend roughly
13. bedizen: to clothe
14. troll: to fish
15. toy: to trifle
16. screen: to protect
17. aver: to assert
18. tamp: to pack
19. yaw: to turn

20. paw: to grasp
21. gutter: to burn
22. sputter: to speak explosively
23. leer: to ogle
24. sheer: to swerve
25. gibbet: to ridicule
26. palter: to bicker
27. breast: to confront
28. blandish: to coax
29. brandish: to flaunt
30. founder: to collapse
31. skewer: to pierce
32. purloin: to steal
33. imbibe: to drink
34. eke: to make with difficulty
35. muster: to gather
36. mulct: to rob
37. animadvert: to criticize
38. quail: to lose courage
39. roil: to stir up
40. bilk: to deceive
41. shunt: to move to one side
42. skulk: to sneak
43. suborn: to bribe
44. extirpate: to destroy
45. pare: to prune
46. incarcerate: to jail
47. countermand: to cancel
48. trek: to travel
49. vitiate: to corrupt
50. enfranchise: to set free
51. cachinnate: to laugh

Adjectives

1. illusive: deceiving
2. pawky: shrewd
3. wary: cautious
4. inimitable: matchless
5. credible: believable
6. adamant: unyielding
7. inane: silly
8. formidable: threatening
9. amiss: wrong
10. remiss: negligent
11. optimal: best
12. ostensible: apparent
13. squalid: dirty

14. auspicious: favorable
15. infamous: bad
16. effusive: excessive
17. audacious: bold
18. swarthy: dark
19. illimitable: infinite
20. equitable: fair
21. germane: fitting
22. benign: harmless
23. fervent: impassioned
24. bereaved: left alone
25. rustic: rural
26. ruthless: cruel
27. sacrosanct: unquestioned
28. taboo: unacceptable
29. surly: testy
30. grueling: demanding
31. vulnerable: open to hurt
32. blatant: obtrusive
33. indulgent: lenient
34. superficial: shallow
35. bleak: depressing
36. profuse: bountiful
37. listless: lacking energy
38. incessant: unceasing
39. bogus: not genuine
40. bona fide: genuine
41. utilitarian: practical
42. martial: warlike
43. Machiavellian: deceptive
44. bourgeois: typical of the middle class
45. protean: changeable
46. abortive: unsuccessful
47. aberrant: atypical
48. quixotic: impractical
49. absolute: complete
50. absurd: ridiculous
51. saturnine: gloomy
52. abysmal: hopeless
53. tawdry: gaudy
54. complaisant: eager to please
55. accountable: responsible
56. debonair: suave
57. dyspeptic: grouchy
58. acerbic: sour
59. acquisitive: greedy
60. depraved: corrupt

Adjectives

1. florid: flowery
2. limpid: clear
3. littoral: coastal
4. quixotic: impractical
5. truant: absent
6. choleric: temperamental
7. churlish: crude
8. circumspect: cautious
9. dubious: questionable
10. ephemeral: short-lived
11. expedient: practical
12. facetious: humorous
13. halcyon: calm
14. idyllic: carefree
15. irresolute: indecisive
16. laudable: commendable
17. loquacious: talkative
18. voluble: talkative
19. mundane: earthly
20. magnanimous: generous
21. nebulous: vague
22. recalcitrant: unruly
23. salient: notable
24. supercilious: haughty
25. superfluous: unnecessary
26. wanton: without regard for what is right
27. venerable: worthy of respect
28. abstruse: difficult to understand
29. arcane: difficult to understand
30. recondite: difficult to understand
31. brackish: having a salty taste
32. callow: immature
33. egregious: shocking
34. eminent: distinguished
35. foppish: vain
36. impecunious: poor
37. indigent: poor
38. intrepid: fearless
39. jocular: joking
40. maladroit: clumsy
41. maudlin: sentimental

42. mellifluous: sweet sounding
43. nefarious: wicked
44. profligate: wicked
45. propitious: advantageous
46. adventitious: accidental
47. fortuitous: accidental
48. querulous: whining
49. reticent: reluctant to speak
50. turgid: swollen
51. caliber: degree of quality
52. cardinal: most important
53. debonair: courteous
54. fetid: having an offensive smell
55. mephitic: having an offensive smell
56. garish: gaudy
57. hebetude: dullness
58. hoary: white with age
59. improvident: wasteful
60. ineluctable: inevitable

Adjectives

1. inscrutable: not understandable
2. incongruous: out of place
3. motley: having many colors
4. natty: neatly dressed
5. obsolete: out of date
6. ordinate: arranged in regular rows
7. parochial: narrow in scope
8. provincial: narrow in scope
9. squalid: neglected
10. spartan: unadorned
11. svelte: slender
12. unwieldy: clumsy
13. ungainly: clumsy
14. vespertine: pertaining to the evening

15. crepuscular: pertaining to the evening
16. xyloid: woodlike
17. ligneous: woodlike
18. zenithal: upright
19. carnivorous: meat eating
20. mendacious: deceptive
21. mercurial: volatile
22. meretricious: showy
23. mordant: caustic
24. nefarious: wicked
25. odious: hateful
26. peremptory: absolute
27. perfidious: treacherous
28. potable: drinkable
29. prefatory: introductory
30. provident: providing for the future
31. puerile: childish
32. redolent: fragrant
33. roseate: cheerful
34. sapid: good tasting
35. strident: harsh
36. sumptuous: expensive
37. trenchant: incisive
38. untrowable: unbelievable
39. wily: cunning
40. abstemious: moderate in eating
41. abysmal: very bad
42. brindled: streaked with a dark color
43. callow: immature
44. captious: critical
45. caviling: critical
46. desultory: random
47. doughty: brave
48. effusive: overflowing
49. egregious: bad
50. estranged: alienated
51. fatuous: silly
52. fractious: rebellious
53. garish: gaudy
54. germane: pertinent
55. gnarled: twisted
56. hapless: unfortunate
57. hoary: white with age
58. igneous: pertaining to fire
59. immanent: inherent
60. imminent: impending

Adjectives

1. eminent: lofty
2. incommodious: troublesome
3. inured: accustomed
4. lurid: pale and gloomy
5. atavistic: resembling an ancestor
6. quotidian: daily
7. diurnal: daily
8. simian: like an ape
9. bovine: like a cow
10. piscine: like a fish
11. saurian: like a lizard
12. vulpine: like a fox
13. quintessential: typical
14. penultimate: next to last
15. edacious: devouring
16. dispassionate: fair
17. imperious: domineering
18. scabrous: rough
19. hebetudinous: dullness
20. minatory: threatening
21. mum: silent
22. nacreous: pearly
23. orotund: resonant; pompous
24. tawdry: cheap
25. august: majestic
26. saturnine: gloomy
27. randy: lustful
28. salubrious: healthy
29. anon: soon
30. protean: changeable
31. erst: formerly
32. quixotic: impractical
33. personable: handsome
34. procrustean: drastic
35. irenic: promoting peace
36. bumptious: conceited
37. debonair: suave
38. dyspeptic: grouchy
39. lachrymose: sad
40. convivial: sociable
41. truculent: savage
42. feral: savage
43. sagacious: wise
44. askance: with suspicion
45. circa: about

46. contumelious: rude
47. en masse: as a group
48. helter-skelter: haphazard
49. presumable: supposable
50. sluggish: lazy
51. ardent: passionate
52. fervent: passionate
53. overt: open
54. covert: secret
55. gingerly: careful
56. meticulous: careful
57. amicable: friendly
58. congenial: friendly
59. callous: unfeeling
60. nocturnal: nightly

6

Relationship Words

We hold these truths to be self-evident, that all men are created equal, that they are endowed by their Creator with certain inalienable Rights, that among these are Life, Liberty, and the pursuit of Happiness.

Thomas Jefferson
1743–1826

Now that is eloquent writing with a matchless seasoning of words from a peerless president of the United States of America, Thomas Jefferson. Of course, these words that live in history are found in the Declaration of Independence.

Did you catch the difficult word *inalienable*? It means "that which cannot be taken away." Synonyms include *nontransferable*, *inviolable*, *sacrosanct*, and *indefeasible*.

The following lists are words that relate to other words, or that can be used in place of those words. You'll notice that some of the lists in this chapter have no definitions. These are lists of synonyms, so the definitions are practically the same as the word to which they all relate, and some of the lists contain words from different parts of speech. Learning these lists will help you stretch your mind and also add variety to your language and conversations.

Words Related to the Word *Small*

1. elfin: small and fairy-like
2. trifling: of little importance
3. infinitesimal: too small to measure
4. picayune: petty
5. lilliputian: small
6. minimize: to reduce
7. minutiae: the small details
8. bantam: small
9. peccadillo: a small fault
10. succinct: brief
11. laconic: using few words
12. abridge: to shorten
13. truncate: to shorten
14. exiguous: scanty
15. scintilla: a trace
16. diminutive: small

Words Related to the Word *Big*

1. plethora: many
2. myriad: many
3. amplitude: greatness of range
4. voluminous: of great volume
5. lummox: a large, awkward person
6. megalopolis: a heavily populated area
7. teeming: prolific
8. titanic: large

9. vista: a broad view
10. aggrandize: to make bigger
11. magnanimous: big in forgiving
12. apotheosize: to deify
13. epitome: the supreme example
14. apotheosis: the supreme example
15. hyperbole: an exaggeration
16. copious: abundant
17. capacious: roomy
18. munificent: generous
19. august: majestic
20. sundry: various

Words Related to Food and Water

1. comestible: edible
2. edacious: craving great quantities of food
3. epicure: one with fine taste in food
4. gourmet: a connoisseur of good food
5. gourmand: a glutton
6. prandial: pertaining to a meal
7. repast: mealtime
8. corpulent: fat
9. porcine: fat
10. ambrosial: delicious
11. saccharine: sickeningly sweet
12. cloying: sickeningly sweet
13. oleaginous: oily
14. masticate: to chew
15. potable: drinkable
16. quaff: to drink heartily
17. sated: full
18. gustatory: pertaining to taste

Words Related to the Word *Bad*

1. baleful: sinister
2. dyspeptic: grouchy
3. bellicose: warlike
4. deleterious: harmful
5. noxious: harmful
6. bilious: bitter
7. pernicious: harmful
8. dissolute: immoral
9. profligate: immoral
10. acidulous: sour
11. bumptious: self-centered
12. parsimonious: stingy
13. captious: critical
14. miscreant: a bad person
15. calamitous: causing calamity
16. churlish: rude
17. boorish: rude
18. contumely: rude actions
19. malefic: evil
20. crotchety: ill-tempered

Words Related to the Word *Happy*

1. exultant
2. exhilarated
3. exuberant
4. euphoric
5. ecstatic
6. blithe
7. gleeful
8. merry
9. hearty
10. providential
11. felicity
12. propitious
13. felicitous
14. jubilant
15. auspicious
16. gay
17. opportune
18. jubilation
19. on top of the world
20. on cloud nine

Words Related to the Word *Rude*

1. impolite
2. impertinent
3. impudent
4. insolent
5. saucy
6. brusque
7. curt
8. uncouth
9. boorish
10. churlish
11. loutish
12. artless
13. inartistic
14. ribald
15. bawdy
16. ungallant
17. uncivil
18. flippant
19. ill-bred
20. surly

Words Related to the Word *Large*

1. cyclopean
2. spacious
3. voluminous
4. ample
5. brawny
6. strapping
7. burly
8. ponderous
9. hulking
10. thumping
11. whopping
12. corpulent
13. rotund
14. portly
15. plump
16. immense
17. capacious
18. hefty
19. solid
20. hunky

Words Related to the Word *Stubborn*

1. intractable
2. intransigent
3. recalcitrant
4. impenetrable
5. restive
6. obstinate
7. obdurate
8. adamant
9. impervious
10. incorrigible
11. unyielding
12. inflexible
13. mulish
14. tenacious
15. pertinacious
16. dogged
17. refractory
18. perverse
19. inflexible
20. wayward

Words Related to the Word *Anger*

1. pique
2. spleen
3. wrath
4. ire
5. enrage
6. infuriate
7. incense
8. gall
9. empurple
10. vex
11. nettle
12. exasperate
13. provoke
14. fury
15. antagonism
16. indignation
17. annoyance
18. outrage
19. irritate
20. mad

Words Related to the Word *Diligent*

1. assiduous
2. sedulous
3. scrupulous
4. meticulous
5. punctilious
6. fastidious
7. pertinacious
8. zealous
9. industrious
10. attentive
11. steadfast
12. hardworking
13. conscientious
14. intent
15. steady
16. persistent
17. earnest
18. painstaking
19. concentrated
20. operose

Words Related to the Word *Sad*

1. lachrymose
2. melancholy
3. lugubrious
4. crestfallen
5. woebegone
6. somber
7. dreary
8. morose
9. gloomy
10. lamentable
11. deplorable
12. shabby
13. forlorn
14. dispirited
15. dejected
16. despondent
17. misery
18. desolate
19. dismal
20. chapfallen

Words Related to the Word *Expert*

1. maven
2. pundit
3. savant
4. virtuoso
5. adept
6. proficient
7. adroit
8. dexterous
9. champion
10. connoisseur
11. wizard
12. masterful
13. superb
14. superior
15. crackerjack
16. specialist
17. skillful
18. knowledgeable
19. practiced
20. accomplished

Words Related to the Word *Good*

1. philanthropist: a charitable person
2. adept: skilled
3. auspicious: favorable
4. propitious: favorable
5. altruistic: unselfish
6. blithe: cheerful
7. proficient: competent
8. salutary: healthful
9. beneficent: doing good
10. amiable: good-natured
11. amity: friendship
12. amicable: friendly
13. concord: agreement
14. felicity: a pleasing manner
15. patrician: nobility
16. paean: a song of praise
17. honorable: worthy of respect
18. obliging: willing to help
19. decorous: dignified
20. admirable: deserving admiration

7

An Assortment of Words

Let all bitterness, wrath, anger, clamor, and evil speaking
be put away from you, with all malice. And be kind to one
another, tenderhearted, forgiving one another, even as God
in Christ forgave you.

Ephesians 4:31–32

How knowledgeable are you about synonyms for various words?

The English language has a plethora of words dealing with various nuances and synonyms of anger, and by contrast, it has a relative paucity of words regarding the munificence of humankind. The above passage details some of the words representing anger. *Clamor* is one such word; it means "vehement protest."

Other synonyms for anger are *antagonism, choler, fury, indignation, ire, irritation, outrage, pique, rage,* and *vexation.*

As you learn these various terms, you can distinguish the subtle nuances of meaning between them. By learning an array of synonyms for various words and by using a dictionary, the particular nuance of any word in question might be better elucidated. Exercising these terms can help you also in relationships, as you are able to better communicate your true meaning.

Incidentally, the book of Ephesians referenced here was written by the apostle Paul and is one of the Epistles in the Bible. An *epistle* is a literary work in the form of a series of letters.

● ● ●

The following lists include a variety of many types of words, all of which will increase your vocabulary considerably. When you begin to understand and use them, you'll find people around you inquiring about their meaning. Then you can help them learn something too!

An Assortment of Words

1. disquisition: a discussion
2. treatise: a discussion
3. thesis: a discussion
4. probity: honesty
5. puissant: powerful
6. comity: courtesy
7. putative: supposed
8. reputed: supposed
9. troglodyte: a cave dweller
10. badinage: joking
11. contretemps: an embarrassing situation
12. sanguine: cheerful
13. apodictic: certain
14. machination: a plot
15. osculation: a kiss

16. abridge: to shorten
17. lute: a primitive guitar
18. timbrel: a primitive tambourine
19. extant: still existing
20. extinct: not existing
21. parsimonious: stingy
22. pulchritude: beauty
23. recrudescence: a revival
24. deipnosophist: a conversationalist
25. emolument: wages
26. crotchet: a whim
27. intrepid: brave
28. vigilant: watchful
29. avid: eager
30. inadvertent: heedless
31. prance: to dance around
32. meniscus: the top surface of a liquid
33. stanchion: an upright pole
34. pitch: to slant
35. hitch: to knot
36. synod: church officials
37. apostrophe: an address to an absent person
38. compeer: a peer
39. scepter: a symbol of authority
40. proviso: an addition to a document
41. plinth: a pedestal
42. jamb: a vertical support
43. girder: a horizontal support
44. flat: an apartment
45. erst: formerly
46. tumbrel: a cart
47. loath: reluctant
48. loathe: to hate
49. ominous: threatening
50. wimple: the attire of a nun
51. diadem: a sign of royalty
52. colophon: the final section of a book
53. pang: a pain
54. jape: a joke

55. mortarboard: a graduation headpiece
56. carpe diem: seize the day
57. tempus fugit: time flies
58. proclivity: an inclination
59. aleatory: depending on chance
60. stool pigeon: an informer

An Assortment of Words

1. thiamin: vitamin B_1
2. riboflavin: vitamin B_2
3. ascorbic acid: vitamin C
4. chalice: a goblet
5. lang syne: bygone days
6. euphemism: a less offensive term
7. incongruous: inappropriate
8. brash: impudent
9. rampant: unchecked
10. intrinsic: inherent
11. ilk: type
12. rue: to regret
13. impasse: a deadlock
14. ignoble: dishonorable
15. idyllic: simple
16. fray: a fight
17. orotund: pompous
18. furbish: to renovate
19. remiss: negligent
20. vouchsafe: to grant
21. inane: silly
22. intrepid: fearless
23. inadvertent: heedless
24. droll: amusing
25. preclude: to prevent
26. temporize: to delay
27. mandate: a command
28. interloper: an unauthorized person
29. demure: modest
30. demur: to object
31. decry: to denounce
32. descry: to catch sight of

33. salient: prominent
34. fillip: an incentive
35. juggernaut: an irresistible force
36. mollify: to soothe
37. nascent: developing
38. inchoate: developing
39. desultory: aimless
40. eleemosynary: supported by charity
41. facile: effortless
42. dissolute: immoral
43. profligate: immoral
44. contumelious: abusive
45. termagant: a violent woman
46. virago: a violent woman
47. harpy: a violent woman
48. eschew: to avoid
49. mercenary: working for money
50. venal: open to bribery
51. nubile: beautiful
52. pugnacious: inclined to fight
53. truculent: inclined to fight
54. peregrination: a journey
55. Promethean: boldly original or daring
56. stygian: gloomy
57. scabrous: obscene
58. scatological: having to do with obscenity
59. scurrilous: obscene
60. concur: to agree

An Assortment of Words

1. admonish: to warn
2. flagrant: very bad
3. duplicity: trickery
4. impunity: freedom from punishment
5. mordant: sarcastic
6. decamp: to go away suddenly
7. pulverulent: powderlike

8. maudlin: sentimental

9. nugatory: trifling

10. avuncular: like an uncle

11. obstreperous: difficult to control

12. ribald: vulgar

13. odious: deserving of hatred

14. ratiocinate: to reason

15. hebetudinous: dull

16. prosaic: dull

17. nescient: ignorant

18. quodlibet: a subtle point of debate

19. sagacious: wise

20. pedantic: showy about learning

21. perspicuity: lucidity

22. perspicacious: perceptive

23. quaff: to drink heartily

24. luminary: a person of eminence

25. palatial: like a palace

26. untrammeled: unrestrained

27. ophidian: snakelike

28. ruck: a large quantity

29. svelte: slender

30. plumb: vertical

31. atavism: resemblance to an ancestor

32. betimes: early

33. pixilated: unbalanced mentally

34. aficionado: a fan

35. subliminal: subconscious

36. largo: a very slow tempo in music

37. adagio: a slow tempo in music

38. andante: a moderate tempo in music

39. freemasonry: brotherhood

40. obfuscate: to confuse

41. protean: changeable

42. bravado: boldness to impress

43. affluent: rich

44. sally: to rush forward

45. consternation: dismay

46. perfunctory: done without care

47. chagrin: humiliation

48. dalliance: flirting
49. cant: insincere statements
50. cardinal: chief
51. carnage: a massacre
52. carrion: dead flesh
53. cataract: waterfall
54. catholic: universal
55. cavort: to prance
56. chattel: moveable property
57. cipher: a zero
58. circumspect: cautious
59. claque: a group hired to applaud
60. comity: civility

An Assortment of Words

1. collate: to assemble in proper order
2. contretemps: an embarrassing event
3. conundrum: a puzzle
4. coterie: a circle of friends
5. dawdle: to delay
6. temporize: to delay
7. defame: to slander
8. disparage: to belittle
9. masticate: to chew
10. voluble: talkative
11. dubious: doubtful
12. forthwith: immediately
13. aleatoric: random
14. argent: silvery
15. auriferous: containing gold
16. austral: southern
17. disparate: different
18. ergo: hence
19. progenitor: ancestor
20. venal: able to be bought
21. vicissitude: a change
22. quicksilver: changeable
23. quintessence: essential
24. scion: a descendant
25. shalom: hello; goodbye; welcome
26. sodality: a club
27. solecism: an error
28. solon: a legislator

29. tautology: a repetition
30. carrion: dead flesh
31. cavort: to strut
32. chattel: moveable property
33. oust: to eject
34. revert: to return
35. emaciated: thin
36. ascend: to rise
37. besiege: to surround
38. pundit: an expert
39. proxy: the authority to act for another
40. prowess: bravery
41. profess: to insincerely lay claim to
42. gambit: a calculated move
43. joust: to combat
44. largo: a very slow movement in music
45. numismatist: a coin collector
46. oleaginous: oily
47. ombudsman: an advocate
48. otiose: futile
49. palaestra: an arena
50. patina: a film formed on statues
51. penultimate: next to the last
52. peregrination: a journey
53. peripatetic: itinerant
54. pseudonym: a pen name
55. panjandrum: a bigwig
56. parley: a conference between enemies
57. pied: multicolored
58. sinister: evil
59. privation: poor
60. ubiquitous: everywhere

An Assortment of Words

1. harbinger: a forerunner
2. respite: an interval of rest

3. raconteur: a story-teller

4. ascertain: to find out definitely

5. ablution: a cleaning

6. adduce: to give as proof

7. affectation: false behavior to impress

8. annotation: an explanatory note

9. appurtenance: an accessory

10. archipelago: a group of islands

11. arrant: notoriously bad

12. auspices: sponsorship

13. bathos: overly sentimental

14. malfeasance: an illegal act by a public official

15. moot: of no practical significance

16. odyssey: a long journey

17. philanderer: a flirt

18. philippic: a harsh attack

19. plebiscite: a vote by everyone

20. renascent: rising again to vigor

21. repartee: a witty exchange

22. riposte: a retort

23. bigot: a narrow-minded person

24. spew: to vomit

25. blatant: showy

26. virulent: harmful

27. astute: keen

28. anon: soon

29. demure: proper

30. dudgeon: resentment

31. effusion: gushing

32. fatuous: foolish

33. fecund: fruitful

34. fraternize: to socialize

35. glabrous: hairless

36. indeterminate: vague

37. indolent: lazy

38. inter: to bury

39. largesse: generosity

40. meretricious: gaudy

41. métier: a vocation

42. misprision: treason
43. mortify: to humiliate
44. plenitude: plenty
45. pyrotechnics: fireworks
46. salinize: to make salty
47. elysian: heavenly
48. inclement: stormy
49. desist: to cease
50. wan: pale
51. elusive: evasive
52. inundate: to flood
53. syncretism: reconciling different beliefs
54. esurient: ravenous
55. bane: a cause of ruin
56. theodicy: divine justice
57. emendation: a correction of errors
58. bijou: jewelry
59. epicene: unmanly
60. sectarian: narrow-minded

An Assortment of Words

1. divertissement: a diversion
2. bonhomie: good-natured
3. metaphor: a figure of speech
4. tendentious: biased
5. terpsichorean: pertaining to dancing
6. poignant: moving
7. corroborate: to confirm
8. obviate: to eliminate
9. quip: a joke
10. placard: a poster
11. disdain: contempt
12. drone: to talk on and on
13. dubious: doubtful
14. eclectic: drawn from many sources
15. engender: to produce
16. erudite: scholarly
17. exigent: urgent

18. extol: to praise
19. facetious: humorous
20. fallacious: false
21. fecund: fertile
22. flagrant: bad
23. forbear: to abstain
24. frenetic: frantic
25. furtive: secretive
26. gainsay: to deny
27. garrulous: talkative
28. genre: an artistic category
29. guile: deceit
30. hermetic: airtight
31. hone: to sharpen
32. impervious: impenetrable
33. impugn: to attack
34. inadvertent: without intention
35. inchoate: developing
36. abstemious: sparing in eating and drinking
37. accolade: praise
38. acquiesce: to agree
39. alacrity: liveliness
40. amiable: friendly
41. apocryphal: false
42. arid: dry or dull
43. assuage: to pacify
44. astute: intelligent
45. audacity: boldness
46. auspicious: promising
47. axiom: a self-evident truth
48. blithe: cheerful
49. brook: to tolerate
50. cognizant: perceptive
51. contempt: disdain
52. contrite: remorseful
53. conundrum: a puzzle
54. credulous: gullible
55. dearth: a scarcity
56. depravity: moral corruption
57. diffident: timid
58. discomfit: to frustrate
59. disinterested: unbiased
60. disparate: different

An Assortment of Words

1. indignant: angry
2. indolence: laziness
3. ineluctable: unavoidable
4. inept: incompetent
5. inevitable: unavoidable
6. infamous: wicked
7. ingenuous: naïve
8. innocuous: harmless
9. insipid: dull
10. intransigent: stubborn
11. jeopardy: danger
12. levity: frivolity
13. lucid: clear
14. maverick: a rebel
15. meander: to wander
16. munificent: generous
17. neophyte: a beginner
18. obdurate: stubborn
19. orthodox: adhering to established doctrines
20. panegyric: praise
21. parsimony: stinginess
22. paucity: scarcity
23. pedagogue: a teacher
24. pedestrian: common
25. penchant: a liking
26. petulant: rude
27. piquant: exciting
28. placid: calm
29. polemic: an argument
30. preclude: to prevent
31. pristine: pure
32. prodigal: wasteful
33. propinquity: nearness
34. provincial: limited
35. prosaic: dull
36. pundit: an expert
37. rampart: a fortification
38. recalcitrant: stubborn
39. refute: to disprove
40. relegate: to assign to an inferior position
41. repudiate: to deny
42. respite: a rest
43. revere: to worship
44. sagacious: wise
45. salubrious: promoting health
46. sanction: to approve

47. spurious: false
48. surreptitious: secret
49. tacit: not spoken
50. temerity: boldness
51. timbre: the quality of sound
52. welter: a turmoil
53. willful: stubborn
54. zealous: fervent
55. supernal: heavenly
56. infernal: detestable
57. effete: weak
58. epicene: effeminate
59. jejune: dull
60. annual: yearly

An Assortment of Words

1. tumid: swollen
2. turgid: swollen
3. turbid: muddy
4. enjoin: to forbid
5. mundane: commonplace
6. curry: to flatter
7. blithe: happy
8. gambol: to skip
9. asperity: harshness of temper
10. interdict: to forbid
11. sanction: to approve
12. gambit: a calculated move
13. bumptious: arrogant
14. discalced: barefoot
15. unsullied: untarnished
16. deft: skilled
17. imbue: to fill
18. imbrue: to stain as with blood
19. dint: a blow
20. stentorian: loud
21. louse: an indecent person
22. sacrosanct: sacred
23. reverie: a daydream
24. educe: to elicit
25. generic: general
26. crepuscular: of twilight

27. matutinal: of morning
28. sartorial: of tailored clothes
29. bespoke: custom-made
30. boor: a rude person
31. churl: a rude person
32. mordant: caustic
33. rake: a scoundrel
34. effluvium: an offensive smell
35. mephitis: an offensive smell
36. welter: wild disorder
37. élan: enthusiasm
38. éclat: a brilliant display
39. misprize: to despise
40. nominal: slight
41. premise: a hypothesis
42. surmise: to guess
43. aspire: to desire
44. raze: to destroy
45. turpitude: depravity
46. exigent: urgent
47. discrete: distinct
48. bevy: a group of animals
49. menagerie: a group of animals
50. evince: to show
51. don: to put on
52. doff: to take off
53. accost: to greet
54. affront: to attack
55. assail: to attack
56. impugn: to attack
57. cavalier: arrogant
58. catamaran: a boat
59. impel: to force
60. vintage: old

An Assortment of Words

1. supervene: to follow
2. rabble: a disorganized crowd
3. horde: a crowd
4. throng: a crowd
5. protean: taking many forms
6. singular: extraordinary

7. sinecure: an easy job

8. stentorian: loud

9. recant: to recall

10. reliction: recession of water

11. stalwart: strong

12. dyspeptic: grouchy

13. prolix: wordy

14. lambent: radiant

15. pulchritudinous: marked by beauty

16. dastardly: mean

17. rogue: a dishonest person

18. knave: a dishonest person

19. proxy: a delegate

20. aplomb: self-assurance

21. aegis: sponsorship

22. pococurante: indifferent

23. mien: appearance

24. denigrate: to defame

25. persiflage: frivolous talk

26. disconsolate: sad

27. tempestuous: stormy

28. imprimatur: official approval

29. facultative: optional

30. declaim: to speak loudly

31. extrinsic: foreign

32. fetter: to hamper

33. nomadic: wandering

34. indigenous: native

35. cosmology: the study of the universe

36. nonplussed: puzzled

37. in extremis: near death

38. fungible: interchangeable

39. ampere: a unit for measuring electricity

40. sui generis: unparalleled

41. enfilade: gunfire

42. purveyor: supplier of food

43. summarily: promptly

44. presently: soon

45. ingrate: an ungrateful person

46. litany: a repetitive recital
47. roseate: optimistic
48. tawny: brownish yellow
49. rubicund: reddish
50. swarthy: dark complexioned
51. harlequin: multicolored
52. ebony: dark
53. parlance: a manner of speaking
54. personable: attractive
55. interloper: an unauthorized person
56. bulwark: protection
57. antithesis: opposite
58. embellish: to adorn
59. cache: a hiding place
60. tony: stylish

An Assortment of Words

1. frippery: showiness
2. inviolable: indestructible
3. distaff: having to do with maternal lineage
4. flange: a projecting edge
5. byzantine: complex
6. analogue: something similar
7. riff: a repeated melodic pattern
8. lulu: anything remarkable
9. frisson: a shudder
10. derisory: ridiculous
11. propriety: the quality of being proper
12. determinate: distinct
13. palpable: obvious
14. reprise: repetition
15. elision: omission of a syllable
16. brio: liveliness
17. solicitude: concern
18. plangent: reverberating
19. factoid: false information

20. amorous: loving
21. impeccable: faultless
22. labyrinth: a maze
23. attest: to certify
24. deploy: to position forces
25. disheveled: untidy
26. loquacious: talkative
27. cognizant: aware
28. prevalent: widespread
29. archaic: antiquated
30. lackluster: dull
31. hierarchy: a system of ranking
32. edict: a decree
33. dictum: a decree
34. infidel: a nonbeliever
35. bona fide: genuine
36. gentry: well bred
37. ablution: a cleansing
38. somber: dismal
39. interlocution: dialogue
40. luminous: brilliant
41. malign: to slander
42. matron: a married woman
43. innate: inborn
44. foretell: to predict
45. inclement: foul
46. languid: fatigued
47. audacious: bold
48. vicarious: indirect
49. vivacious: spirited
50. putsch: a plot
51. jejune: dull
52. cupidity: greed
53. ghee: liquid butter
54. ragout: a stew
55. penuche: candy
56. folderol: foolish talk
57. mauve: bluish purple
58. gibe: to jeer
59. accord: an agreement
60. invoke: to call
61. veracious: truthful
62. animus: anger
63. animadversion: criticism

Phobia (Fear-of) Words

Phobia is Latin for "the fear of something."

1. agoraphobia: open spaces
2. androphobia: men
3. arachnophobia: spiders
4. astrophobia: thunder and lightning
5. acrophobia: high places
6. claustrophobia: closed spaces
7. hydrophobia: water
8. russophobia: Russians
9. triskaidekaphobia: the number thirteen
10. xenophobia: strangers
11. brontephobia: thunder and lightning
12. cynophobia: dogs
13. herpetophobia: reptiles
14. ophidiophobia: snakes
15. homophobia: homosexuals
16. necrophobia: death
17. nyctophobia: darkness
18. pyrophobia: fire
19. sitophobia: food
20. ataxophobia: disorder

Ology (Study-of) Words

Ology is Latin for "the study of."

1. anthropology: humans
2. archaeology: past human cultures
3. axiology: values
4. bacteriology: bacteria
5. biology: living organisms
6. cosmology: the universe

7. cryptology: codes
8. cytology: cells
9. deontology: ethics
10. enology: wines
11. entomology: insects
12. epistemology: the limits of knowledge
13. eschatology: the end of the world
14. etiology: causes
15. etymology: words
16. geology: earth
17. gerontology: aging
18. hagiology: saints
19. herpetology: reptiles
20. histology: living tissue
21. horology: time
22. ichthyology: fish
23. kinesiology: motion
24. mammalogy: mammals
25. morphology: structure
26. mycology: fungi
27. numismatology: coins
28. oncology: cancer
29. ophthalmology: eyes
30. ornithology: birds
31. paleontology: fossils
32. parasitology: parasites
33. pathology: diseases
34. philology: language
35. physiology: the functions of living organisms
36. sociology: the origin and development of human society
37. teleology: final causes
38. thanatology: death
39. toxicology: poisons
40. zoology: animals

8

Various Nuances of Sundry Words

Use the right word and not its second cousin.

Mark Twain
1835–1910

One of the most beloved novelists in American history is Mark Twain. He had a way with the nuances of words. Who does not remember bygone days of laughing at *The Adventures of Tom Sawyer* or *The Adventures of Huckleberry Finn*? Twain had a brilliant command of the English language. Knowing the exact word to use can come only from precise knowledge and reflects mental brilliance.

Various Synonyms Giving Nuances of Meaning

1. maverick: an independent person
2. atavistic: resembling an ancestor
3. matutinal: relating to morning
4. supercilious: proud
5. lothario: a flirt
6. auspices: sponsorship
7. rake: a scoundrel
8. nemesis: an enemy
9. avert: to turn away
10. philippic: criticism
11. churl: a vulgar person
12. bacchanal: a riotous party
13. tawdry: gaudy
14. mar: to damage
15. raze: to demolish
16. rail: to scold
17. boon: a blessing
18. bagatelle: a trifle
19. ballast: a stabilizer
20. virtuoso: a skilled performer
21. baleful: sinister
22. reticence: a quietness
23. effluvium: an offensive smell
24. archipelago: a group of islands
25. annotation: an explanatory note
26. welter: a wild disorder
27. trepidation: fear
28. droll: humorous
29. respite: a rest
30. bumptious: arrogant
31. dyspeptic: grouchy
32. acquisitive: greedy
33. anomie: a lack of social standards
34. redoubtable: formidable
35. éclat: brilliance
36. impel: to force
37. anthology: a collection of artistic works
38. meticulous: particular
39. debonair: suave
40. convivial: sociable
41. misprize: to despise

42. supervene: to follow
43. antipodal: opposite
44. ague: malarial fever
45. abstract: intangible
46. exigent: urgent
47. impugn: to assail
48. cabal: a conspiracy
49. lapidarian: showing elegance
50. caste: a social class system
51. gravity: seriousness
52. cacophony: displeasing noise
53. rabble: a disorderly crowd
54. détente: an easing of tension
55. apostle: a messenger
56. apoplexy: a loss of consciousness
57. inordinate: excessive
58. effete: weak
59. ecumenical: universal
60. rancor: anger

Various Synonyms Giving Nuances of Meaning

1. castigate: to punish
2. sinecure: an easy job
3. jejune: dull
4. insipid: dull
5. apparition: a ghost
6. appurtenance: an accessory
7. temper: to moderate
8. elite: the best
9. whet: to stimulate
10. rapprochement: a reestablishing of relations
11. tumid: swollen
12. enjoin: to forbid
13. scrutinize: to examine closely
14. arpeggio: the rapid playing of successive tones
15. artful: sly

16. artifice: a trick
17. obloquy: slander
18. wince: to flinch
19. artless: crude
20. largo: a very slow tempo
21. copious: abundant
22. evanescent: fleeting
23. alienist: a psychiatrist
24. curry: to flatter
25. recalcitrant: unruly
26. dire: urgent
27. esker: a ridge
28. askew: crooked
29. assail: to attack
30. beadle: a minor official
31. amatory: erotic
32. odyssey: a long, difficult journey
33. bathos: overly sentimental
34. narcissism: egocentrism
35. bazaar: a marketplace
36. Olympian: superior
37. behest: a command
38. innocuous: harmless
39. herald: to greet with enthusiasm
40. aberrant: atypical
41. clandestine: secretive
42. covert: secretive
43. furtive: secretive
44. largess: a gift
45. banal: dull
46. vapid: dull
47. mundane: dull
48. truculent: warlike
49. bellicose: warlike
50. irascible: warlike
51. discordant: warlike
52. manifold: diverse
53. multifarious: diverse
54. eclectic: diverse
55. heterogeneous: diverse
56. lethargic: sluggish
57. torpid: sluggish
58. languid: sluggish
59. astute: clever
60. ingenious: clever

Various Synonyms Giving Nuances of Meaning

1. lucid: clear
2. cogent: clear
3. incisive: clear
4. patent: clear
5. trenchant: clear
6. pellucid: clear
7. mollify: to calm
8. placate: to calm
9. sober: calm
10. placid: calm
11. acclaim: praise
12. adulation: praise
13. accolade: praise
14. approbation: praise
15. kudos: praise
16. extol: to praise
17. laud: to praise
18. ameliorate: to improve
19. ambiguous: vague
20. equivocal: vague
21. diffident: shy
22. timorous: shy
23. emancipate: to free
24. vindicate: to free from blame
25. fallacious: false
26. mendacious: false
27. spurious: false
28. apocryphal: false
29. specious: false
30. assail: to attack
31. beset: to attack
32. censure: to attack
33. berate: to attack
34. revile: to attack
35. inveigh: to attack
36. decry: to attack
37. denigrate: to attack
38. disparage: to attack
39. deprecate: to attack
40. assault: to attack
41. riser: part of a staircase
42. slalom: ski racing
43. gibbet: to ridicule
44. leer: to ogle
45. feckless: useless
46. cloche: a hat
47. brogue: a shoe
48. exploit: a daring achievement

49. tamp: to pack
50. tamper: to meddle
51. yaw: to veer
52. paw: to grope
53. anode: a positively charged electrode
54. cathode: a negatively charged electrode
55. gutter: to burn
56. egress: an exit
57. divagate: to wander
58. jape: a joke
59. vocalic: related to vowels
60. irenic: promoting peace

Various Synonyms Giving Nuances of Meaning

1. rill: a small stream
2. phycology: the study of algae
3. wherefore: why
4. whence: from where
5. dither: a state of indecision
6. hart: a male deer
7. sforzando: an accent on tone
8. passion: intensity of feelings
9. quod vide: which see
10. sine qua non: an indispensable condition
11. anno: year
12. sine: without
13. quod: jail
14. vat: a tank
15. gloaming: dusk
16. palter: to bicker
17. chantey: a song for the sea
18. apothegm: an adage
19. draconian: cruel
20. daguerreotype: a primitive photograph
21. lute: a primitive guitar
22. timbrel: a primitive tambourine
23. recorder: a primitive flute
24. expletive: an oath or swearword

25. exposé: statement of facts
26. lang syne: bygone days
27. chalice: a goblet
28. gewgaw: a trinket
29. stool pigeon: an informer
30. Herodotus: the father of history
31. nosology: the classification of diseases
32. saw: an adage
33. ordinal: a number defining a position, such as fifth
34. cardinal: a number denoting quantity
35. paleology: the study of antiquities
36. physiognomy: the study of faces
37. caliber: the worth of something
38. troll: to fish
39. toy: to trifle
40. divagate: to wander
41. mauve: bluish purple
42. puce: brownish purple
43. escarpment: a steep hill
44. barbican: a type of fortification
45. yaw: to turn
46. paw: to grasp
47. gutter: to burn
48. sputter: to speak quickly
49. leer: to ogle
50. gibbet: to ridicule
51. palter: to quibble
52. blandish: to coax
53. brandish: to flaunt
54. anathema: a loathed person
55. fronds: leaves
56. caesura: pause
57. prelude: the beginning of a musical
58. coda: the final passage in a music movement
59. colophon: the final section of a book
60. festoon: a wreath

Various Synonyms Giving Nuances of Meaning

1. joule: a unit for the measurement of energy
2. newton: a unit for the measurement of force
3. motif: a recurring theme in a novel
4. refrain: a recurring theme in a poem
5. ersatz: a substitute
6. ophidian: pertaining to snakes
7. ornithoid: resembling a bird
8. ichthyolite: a fossil fish
9. diva: a female opera singer
10. laud: praise
11. laird: a landowner
12. abrogate: to cancel
13. esker: a ridge
14. biretta: the head ornament of a priest
15. miter: the head ornament of a bishop
16. protocol: rules of behavior
17. habiliment: rules of dress
18. cloture: a process to end debate
19. cease-fire: a process to end fighting
20. taps: an evening military signal
21. reveille: a morning military signal
22. vespers: evening prayers
23. matins: morning prayers
24. schooner: a ship
25. cruiser: a ship
26. ziggurat: a tower
27. campanile: a bell tower
28. parapet: a low protective wall
29. moorage: a place to tie up a craft
30. hitching post: a place to tie up a horse
31. quidnunc: a busybody
32. exchequer: a national treasury

33. porter: a baggage carrier
34. siphon: a conduit for liquid
35. flue: a conduit for smoke
36. silo: a structure that stores grain
37. mutiny: desertion
38. whet: to sharpen
39. hone: to sharpen
40. wadi: gully
41. cape: a promontory
42. promontory: a bluff or prominent hill
43. cub: a reporter
44. page: a youth training for knighthood
45. plebe: a cadet
46. scuttle: to destroy a ship
47. yeti: the abominable snowman
48. scrawl: to write carelessly
49. bursar: a treasurer at a college
50. matriculation: enrolling at college
51. haze: smoke plus fog
52. lees: sediment
53. beret: a soft, visorless hat
54. derby: a hat
55. fedora: a soft, felt hat
56. pillbox: a small, round hat
57. script: the written text of a play
58. rout: to drive out
59. nosology: the classification of diseases
60. utopia: an imaginary, perfect land

Various Synonyms Giving Nuances of Meaning

1. patronymics: surnames
2. lang syne: bygone days
3. phycology: the study of algae

4. rill: a small stream
5. irenic: promoting peace
6. compeer: a peer
7. current: a unit of energy
8. volt: a unit of electromotive force
9. watt: a unit of electrical power
10. atoll: an island surrounding a lagoon
11. icon: an image
12. riant: cheerful
13. paramount: chief
14. mentor: a teacher
15. tutelage: training
16. impractical: speculative
17. impracticable: not capable of being done
18. equus: a horse
19. bos: a cow
20. atelier: a studio
21. durance: imprisonment
22. privy: a toilet
23. ecophobia: fear of home
24. prepossessing: attractive
25. boreal: north
26. entre nous: in confidence
27. fiat: an order
28. habiliment: attire
29. demur: to delay
30. ersatz: a substitute
31. balaclava: a hood
32. hauteur: arrogance
33. littoral: pertaining to the shore
34. pelagic: pertaining to the sea
35. torte: a cake
36. tort: injustice
37. stomata: a pore
38. strait: a difficult situation
39. vendible: corrupt
40. venal: corrupt
41. polemic: an argument
42. quintessence: purest example

43. magenta: purplish red
44. cyan: greenish blue
45. canard: a rumor
46. dote: to fancy
47. decry: to disparage
48. natatorium: a swimming pool
49. naupathia: seasickness
50. pall: to lose power
51. pansophism: universal knowledge
52. paroxysm: a fit
53. cacography: bad handwriting
54. peremptory: dictatorial
55. persiflage: teasing
56. presumptuous: bold
57. promulgate: to publish
58. rectitude: honesty
59. sibyl: a fortune-teller
60. sobriquet: a nickname

Various Synonyms Giving Nuances of Meaning

1. stultify: to make to appear stupid
2. stupefaction: a stunned state
3. lagniappe: a gift
4. trumpery: something showy
5. vertiginous: dizzy
6. votary: a person bound by vows
7. abecedarian: a beginner
8. preternatural: supernatural
9. requital: the act of repaying
10. regale: to entertain in a lavish manner
11. puissant: powerful
12. profundity: depth of thought
13. placate: to appease
14. apocryphal: of doubtful authenticity
15. baccalaureate: a bachelor's degree
16. polity: a system of government

17. bohemian: unconventional
18. graft: corruption
19. brandish: to present ostentatiously
20. miscegenation: inter-breeding
21. mortify: to humiliate
22. brassy: bold
23. cartel: a coalition for control
24. bemused: the state of being perplexed
25. confabulate: to chit-chat
26. annunciate: to announce
27. consternation: alarm
28. Babbitt: a materialistic person
29. discombobulate: to confuse
30. disport: to play
31. bedraggled: unkempt
32. efflorescent: blossoming
33. enshrine: to cherish
34. conjure: to bring about
35. consortium: an alliance
36. eviscerate: to disembowel
37. fabulist: a liar
38. hardtack: a biscuit
39. feral: wild
40. titillate: to arouse
41. flimflam: a swindle
42. foray: an initial attempt
43. testator: a male with a will
44. testatrix: a female with a will
45. globular: globe shaped
46. grope: to act with uncertainty
47. hapless: unlucky
48. comport: to bring together
49. hominid: human
50. shibboleth: a widely held belief
51. immolate: to kill
52. dank: damp and cold
53. incarnate: embodied
54. inculpate: to incriminate

55. fop: a vain person
56. maraud: to loot
57. inertia: lack of energy
58. inimical: harmful
59. kibosh: the act of stopping
60. liturgy: a ritual of worship

Various Synonyms Giving Nuances of Meaning

1. palaver: a parley
2. parlance: a manner of speaking
3. torte: a cake
4. tort: a civil misdeed
5. solipsism: self-centeredness
6. stultify: to cause to look foolish
7. maniacal: insane
8. garrulity: talkativeness
9. pander: a pimp
10. benighted: unenlightened
11. bluster: to threaten
12. napalm: a weapon of burning plastic
13. Neolithic: of the Stone Age
14. opine: to state one's view
15. pagination: the sequence of pages
16. megalomania: delusions of grandeur
17. ingrate: an ungrateful person
18. desideratum: something desired
19. patrimony: a legacy
20. persnickety: fussy
21. narcoma: a coma from narcotics
22. physiognomy: the human face
23. nether: lower
24. precipice: a cliff
25. preemptive: possessing a prior right
26. simulacrum: a similarity
27. sobriquet: a nickname

28. primordial: original
29. progenitor: an ancestor
30. solecism: a blunder in speech
31. nom de guerre: a wartime name
32. propagate: to multiply
33. quark: an elementary particle
34. reapportionment: redistribution
35. contrivance: a device
36. reconnoiter: to explore
37. proverbial: showing a parallel with a maxim
38. restive: uneasy
39. numerology: foreseeing the future through numbers
40. semantics: the way something is phrased
41. temblor: an earthquake
42. serendipitous: accidental
43. sociometry: the study of social differences
44. hotspur: a hotheaded person
45. imbue: to saturate
46. solicitous: worried
47. soliloquy: a monologue
48. stymie: to hinder
49. purlieus: a neighborhood
50. sully: to soil
51. surcease: a cessation
52. syllogism: an argument with three propositions
53. tandem: one after another
54. haute couture: high fashion
55. hegemony: undue influence
56. terra cotta: clay pottery
57. Tetragrammaton: God
58. canard: a false story
59. tintinnabulation: the ringing of bells
60. torrential: pertaining to severe storms

Various Synonyms Giving Nuances of Meaning

1. plethora: many
2. paucity: fewness
3. asperity: roughness of manner
4. amenity: smoothness of manner
5. savant: a learned person
6. sciolist: a person with only superficial knowledge
7. interdict: to forbid
8. imprimatur: to approve
9. enervate: to deprive of energy
10. energize: to give energy
11. prolix: wordy
12. pithy: concise
13. infinite: endless
14. infinitesimal: too small to measure
15. salubrious: wholesome
16. saturnine: gloomy
17. contentious: argumentative
18. civil: polite
19. concur: to agree
20. cavil: to disagree
21. incursion: an attack
22. rail: to attack
23. revilement: an attack
24. denigration: an attack
25. disparagement: an attack
26. rife: abundant
27. profuse: abundant
28. replete: abundant
29. inundation: an abundance
30. opulence: an abundance
31. surfeit: an abundance
32. plethora: an abundance
33. insidious: harmful
34. defamatory: harmful
35. deleterious: harmful
36. noxious: harmful
37. buttress: to support
38. bolster: to support
39. ecstatic: happy
40. dour: sad

9

Difficult Words

There was a man in the land of Uz, whose name was Job; and that man was perfect and upright, and one that feared God, and eschewed evil.

Job 1:1 (KJV)

Is the word *eschew* one you would like to eschew?

The word *eschew* may perplex many people. *Eschew* means "to avoid, to abstain from, to keep clear of, to shun."

Job is a fascinating book in the Old Testament. One of the major books of wisdom literature in the Bible, it differs from the others because it uses a number of genres and has unusual grammatical construction. The book of Job, written circa 2000 BC, has fascinated readers for centuries. A number of rare and difficult words that appeared in the original Hebrew language are used by the author.

An excellent vocabulary helps us understand today's translations in comprehending such terms as *eschew, land of Uz, Chaldeans, sanctify, wrath, Sheol, tumult, Behemoth, pinions, Pleiades,* and *Orion*—all found in this ancient book of wisdom literature.

If more people read literature and Scripture, doubtless they would glean so much more knowledge to apply to all areas of their lives.

Only the upper 5 to 10 percent of the population know the words in the following lists. They are indeed difficult words. Learn them and go where only brilliant minds have gone.

An Assortment of Difficult Words

1. surd: voiceless
2. petroglyph: a prehistoric carving
3. obelisk: a tapering column
4. pulsar: a collapsed star of high density
5. umbra: the dark center of a sunspot
6. abiosis: the absence of life
7. arboreal: pertaining to trees
8. fruticose: shrublike
9. ligneous: woodlike
10. verdant: green
11. arrears: a debt
12. exchequer: a national treasury
13. mitigate: to make less severe
14. proxy: the authority to act for another
15. tort: a noncriminal wrongful act
16. batten: to reinforce
17. bevel: a non–right angle
18. immurement: confinement within walls

19. peculation: misuse of public money
20. eolian: affected by wind
21. subliminal: beneath consciousness
22. atomism: a society of distinct factions
23. solecism: a violation of accepted language
24. telesis: planned progress
25. humic: from the soil
26. pedology: the study of soils
27. pluvial: drizzly
28. viand: a dish of food
29. caldera: a volcanic crater
30. lotic: pertaining to flowing water
31. riparian: pertaining to a riverbank
32. atoll: a coral island
33. alpine: pertaining to mountains
34. igneous: pertaining to fire
35. apparat: the existing power structure
36. thralldom: slavery
37. parlance: a manner of expressing oneself
38. pidgin: a mixture of languages
39. analects: a literary passage
40. colophon: a publisher's emblem
41. fustian: bombastic writing
42. missive: a letter
43. vignette: a short story
44. ostinato: a repeated melodic pattern
45. canon: a tenet that is consistent and logical
46. anaclitic: dependent on another person
47. dereistic: not in reality
48. moor: to anchor a ship
49. regatta: a boat race
50. anagogic: relating to lofty ideas
51. foray: a raid

52. troubadour: a poet of the medieval period
53. immanent: inherent
54. joule: a unit of energy
55. idiotropic: introspective
56. surgent: rising
57. predicant: a preacher
58. ableism: discrimination against the disabled
59. loge: a balcony
60. labefaction: a weakening of morality

An Assortment of Difficult Words

1. scrim: a curtain
2. docent: a tour guide
3. compendium: a sketch
4. apiary: a place where bees are kept
5. aviary: a place where birds are kept
6. vespiary: a place where wasps are kept
7. pabulum: nourishment for an animal
8. anthology: a collection of writings
9. ullage: an empty space in a tank for water
10. involution: taking a number to a power
11. vellicate: to cause convulsive twitching
12. drivel: nonsense
13. lorry: a truck
14. serviette: a napkin
15. settee: a sofa
16. barmy: frothy
17. bobby: a police officer
18. mackintosh: a raincoat
19. caudillo: a head of state
20. arroyo: a gulch
21. tout le monde: everyone
22. tout de suite: immediately
23. tout à fait: entirely
24. reynard: a fox
25. spinnaker: a large sail

26. vermicelli: thin spaghetti-like pasta
27. argosy: a large merchant ship
28. macadam: a pavement
29. hoyden: a tomboy
30. juggernaut: an overpowering force
31. esquire: a gentleman
32. El Dorado: a wealthy place
33. belfry: a bell tower
34. jackanapes: a whippersnapper
35. nonplus: to puzzle
36. paterfamilias: the male head of a family
37. patronymic: family name or surname
38. Paternoster: the Lord's Prayer
39. animalcule: a microscopic organism
40. animus: hostile feeling
41. inalienable: not transferable to another
42. indefeasible: inalienable
43. ersatz: a fake
44. angst: anxiety
45. echt: authentic
46. verboten: forbidden
47. zeitgeist: the feeling characteristic of an era
48. nosh: a snack
49. tsuris: worries
50. yenta: busybody
51. futon: a mattress
52. shogun: a warlord
53. tycoon: a person of great wealth
54. cyberspace: electronic communication
55. gigabyte: a measure of data storage capacity
56. amicus curiae: a friend of the court
57. pro bono: legal services without a fee
58. quark: elementary particles
59. baryons: elementary particles
60. visceral: physiological

An Assortment of Difficult Words

1. midden: a refuse heap
2. hermitage: a hideaway
3. vestibule: a middle room
4. mezzanine: a low balcony
5. annulet: a ring-shaped ridge
6. aurora: a display of light
7. nebula: an interstellar cloud
8. clastic: causing division into parts
9. detritus: decaying organic matter
10. fruticose: shrublike
11. herbarium: dried plants
12. terrarium: an enclosure for plants
13. scandent: pertaining to climbing growth
14. sylvan: living in the forest
15. specie: money in coins
16. chattel: moveable property
17. demur: to object
18. dowel: a round peg
19. piton: a spike
20. pilfer: to steal
21. recidivism: a return to criminal activity
22. effluent: wastewater
23. littoral: pertaining to the coastline
24. simoom: a dust storm
25. squall: a sudden wind
26. spate: a sudden flood
27. zephyr: a gentle wind
28. calorie: a unit of heat
29. confectionary: any sweet food
30. comestible: edible
31. condiment: a seasoning for food
32. larder: a pantry
33. sieve: to strain
34. tureen: a pot
35. scarp: a cliff

36. chatoyant: having the glow of gems
37. shard: a fragment of glass
38. tufa: a porous rock
39. ombudsman: an intermediary
40. regalia: trappings of a military office
41. pejorative: negative in connotation
42. proem: an introduction
43. sesquipedalian: a very long word
44. speleology: cave exploration
45. sciamachy: shadow boxing
46. chary: careful
47. sans: without
48. minatory: threatening
49. cachet: prestige
50. triturate: to crush
51. doyen: a leader
52. susurrus: a whispering
53. cynosure: the center of attention
54. propinquity: nearness
55. pusillanimous: cowardly
56. hispid: hairy
57. libidinous: characterized by lust
58. miscreant: a villain
59. tergiversation: desertion
60. fainéant: lazy

An Assortment of Difficult Words

1. bête noire: something feared
2. scarify: to hurt the feelings of
3. bon mot: witticism
4. apodictic: certain
5. hebetude: dullness
6. ingenue: an innocent young woman
7. sangfroid: composure
8. gasconade: bragging

9. mot juste: the right word
10. venial: forgivable
11. sine qua non: that which is essential
12. execrate: to denounce
13. éclat: acclaim
14. puissant: strong
15. demarche: a change of policy
16. venal: bribable
17. élan: enthusiasm
18. harpy: a shrewish woman
19. jejune: dull
20. Homeric: epic
21. peculate: to steal
22. paean: a song of praise
23. rectitude: honesty
24. putative: reputed
25. argonaut: an adventurer
26. vernal: springlike
27. disenthrall: to set free
28. troglodyte: a cave dweller
29. terpsichorean: pertaining to dancing
30. acquisitiveness: greed
31. cachinnate: to laugh
32. pleonastic: wordy
33. putsch: a plot to overthrow a government
34. dacha: a country house
35. apothegm: an aphorism
36. ragout: a stew
37. quotidian: daily
38. hauteur: a haughty spirit
39. nacre: mother-of-pearl
40. folderol: foolish talk
41. guano: a natural fertilizer
42. pince-nez: eyeglasses
43. diva: a distinguished female singer
44. mauve: bluish purple
45. defalcation: the misappropriation of money
46. ewer: a pitcher with a wide spout
47. ogle: to look at flirtatiously

48. thespian: an actor
49. argosy: an opulent supply
50. Tartar: a savage person
51. phantasmagoria: deceptive appearances
52. meerschaum: a tobacco pipe
53. maelstrom: a disordered state of affairs
54. horde: a large crowd
55. treacle: something cloying
56. helot: a slave
57. quahog: a clam
58. sylph: a slender woman
59. bluestocking: an intellectual woman
60. mountebank: a charlatan

An Assortment of Difficult Words

1. imbroglio: a difficult situation
2. sylph: a slender woman
3. bluestocking: an intellectual woman
4. mendicant: a beggar
5. tsuris: worries
6. zaftig: plump
7. sarcophagus: a stone coffin
8. siren: a beautiful woman
9. rialto: a shopping center or mart
10. caprice: a sudden change of mind
11. ballyhoo: blatant advertising
12. rake: a dissolute person
13. Arcadian: a simple, rustic person
14. pooh-bah: a self-important person
15. palaver: idle talk
16. toady: a flattering person
17. martinet: a disciplinarian

18. blandishment: flattery
19. deipnosophist: a conversationalist
20. hebdomadal: weekly
21. epigram: a short saying
22. concupiscent: sexually immoral
23. capricious: flighty
24. quotidian: daily
25. interpolate: to insert
26. disquisition: a discussion
27. bowdlerize: to purge
28. importune: demanding
29. bathysiderodromophobia: fear of subways
30. emolument: a salary
31. inalienable: not capable of being taken away
32. peripeteia: a reversal in the action of a play
33. gisant: a sculpture of a deceased person
34. succor: to help
35. triturate: to pulverize
36. wizened: wrinkled
37. carapace: a protective coating
38. screed: a monotonous speech
39. solipsism: self-focus
40. scabrous: scaly
41. sobriquet: a nickname
42. solace: comfort in sorrow
43. senescence: old age
44. subversion: overthrow
45. surrogate: a substitute
46. suborn: to persuade another to crime
47. stygian: gloomy
48. subsistence: existence
49. seine: a fishing net
50. scurrilous: obscene
51. scathed: harmed
52. stentorian: loud
53. sycophant: a flatterer
54. surmount: to overcome
55. strident: harsh sounding
56. solemnity: seriousness
57. inexorable: unyielding
58. intransigent: unyielding

59. implacable: unyielding

60. Sisyphean: requiring endless effort

An Assortment of Difficult Words

1. coruscating: radiant
2. nonage: youth
3. casuistry: guile
4. objurgation: a rebuke
5. bombilation: a buzzing sound
6. conurbation: an urban area
7. Bolshevik: a revolutionary
8. wormwood: something unpleasant
9. blarney: flattery
10. shrew: a tenacious person
11. blitzkrieg: a sudden, all-out attack
12. kibitzer: a meddler
13. nacre: mother-of-pearl
14. weltanschauung: a worldview
15. eremite: hermit
16. anchorite: hermit
17. orthography: study of correct spelling
18. moiety: a portion
19. interpolate: to insert
20. tintinnabulation: the ringing of bells
21. insufferable: intolerable
22. inimitable: matchless
23. ineffable: inexpressible
24. ineluctable: unavoidable
25. eleemosynary: involving charity
26. blandishment: flattery
27. descant: to elaborate
28. feckless: ineffective
29. obtain: to be customary
30. scurvy: despicable
31. plangent: thundering
32. fell: cruel

33. consequential: pompous
34. epicene: effeminate
35. moniker: a nickname
36. hortatory: urging
37. garret: a loft
38. protean: changeable
39. caveat: a warning
40. cavalier: arrogant
41. ragout: a stew
42. bailiwick: one's area of skill
43. folderol: foolish talk
44. plexiform: complicated
45. ewer: a pitcher
46. factitious: false
47. jackanapes: a rude young man
48. nonplus: perplexed
49. fainéant: lazy
50. otiose: lazy
51. hebetudinous: lazy
52. indolent: lazy
53. torpid: lazy
54. chutzpah: brashness
55. nacreous: pearly
56. sub rosa: secretly
57. tergiversation: desertion
58. scurrilous: foul-mouthed
59. scatological: preoccupation with obscenity
60. divagate: to ramble

An Assortment of Difficult Words

1. arrogate: to demand
2. nebbish: a nobody
3. hebdomadal: weekly
4. quotidian: daily
5. doyenne: a senior female member of a group
6. doyen: a senior male member of a group
7. apodictic: certain
8. bonanza: a sudden windfall
9. scarify: to lacerate

10. homunculus: a small person
11. deipnosophist: a conversationalist
12. fulgent: radiant
13. beguine: a dance
14. hebetude: lethargy
15. fanfaronade: bragging
16. inamorata: a female sweetheart
17. droll: laughable
18. immure: to entomb
19. eruct: to belch
20. aleatory: depending on chance
21. putative: supposed
22. threnody: a funeral song
23. pleonasm: a redundancy
24. tautology: a redundancy
25. quidnunc: a busybody
26. imprimatur: sanction
27. pablum: bland food
28. manumit: to emancipate
29. flagitious: wicked
30. iterate: to repeat
31. ontogeny: the development of an organism
32. alogia: using few words
33. aphasia: the loss of ability to speak
34. dishabille: partial undress
35. piebald: spotted
36. phantasm: a ghost
37. specter: a ghost
38. prowess: skill
39. quay: a wharf
40. jetty: a wharf
41. raffish: unconventional
42. rampant: widespread
43. recreant: a coward
44. rectitude: honesty
45. screed: a sermon
46. yaw: to veer
47. sere: dry
48. xeric: dry
49. vitriol: angry remarks
50. sluice: a floodgate

51. slue: to rotate
52. seminal: basic
53. reliquary: a shrine
54. portico: a porch
55. lackey: an assistant
56. oeuvre: lifework
57. nicety: detail
58. buss: to kiss
59. osculate: to kiss
60. echelon: rank

An Assortment of Difficult Words

1. detritus: rubbish
2. bilk: to cheat
3. escarp: a cliff
4. ken: knowledge
5. ineffable: unspeakable
6. importune: to beg
7. imbroglio: a confused situation
8. hovel: a hut
9. melee: a brawl
10. laud: to praise
11. mollify: to calm
12. prate: to chatter
13. portico: a porch
14. quaff: to guzzle
15. dais: a podium
16. rostrum: a podium
17. subtle: elusive
18. urbane: sophisticated
19. debonair: sophisticated
20. stultify: to make foolish
21. sororal: relating to a sister
22. soporific: sleep inducing
23. soigné: fashionable
24. ululate: to howl
25. wizened: wrinkled
26. whet: to sharpen
27. verdant: green
28. angst: anxiety
29. gestalt: perceived whole
30. gaffe: a faux pas
31. de jure: by law
32. nom de plume: a pen name

33. rara avis: a rarity
34. tabula rasa: a blank slate
35. apiculture: beekeeping
36. fabulist: a fraud
37. drivel: nonsense
38. apoplectic: angry
39. dragoon: to intimidate
40. arras: a tapestry
41. devolve: to delegate
42. curate: a clergyman
43. aureole: a halo
44. belay: to secure
45. collier: a coal miner
46. gelid: icy
47. cicatrix: a scar
48. cudgel: a club
49. factotum: an assistant
50. flout: to defy
51. keen: to lament
52. humbug: a fraud
53. mere: a pond
54. macerate: to soften by soaking in liquid

National Spelling Bee–Winning Words

1. eczema: an inflammation of the skin
2. ratoon: a new shoot from a root of sugarcane
3. abalone: a mollusk
4. interlocutory: conversational
5. croissant: a rich, crescent-shaped roll
6. macerate: to waste away
7. vouchsafe: to grant
8. narcolepsy: a disease with times of sudden sleepiness
9. sarcophagus: a stone coffin
10. psoriasis: a skin disease characterized by red patches
11. Purim: a Jewish festival
12. luge: a sled
13. milieu: an environment
14. staphylococci: bacteria

15. spoliator: one who destroys

16. antipyretic: fever-reducing

17. Chihuahua: a small dog

18. hydrophyte: an aquatic plant

19. incisor: a tooth at the front of the mouth

20. deification: being made into a god

10

Prefixes, Suffixes, and Roots

And the LORD God said unto the woman, What is this that thou hast done? And the woman said, The serpent beguiled me, and I did eat.

Genesis 3:13 (KJV)

The word *beguiled* is an interesting word that employs a prefix. The word *guile* means "deceit." The prefix *be* is an intensifier that means "completely."

Ex, another interesting prefix, means "out"; it is found in the word *exodus*, which is also the title of the second book of the Old Testament. An exodus (way out) is the theme of the book. Exodus is the record of the Israelites' deliverance from (or the way out of) Egypt.

●●●

Knowing difficult words is often helpful. And one easy way to increase one's vocabulary is to discover the etymology of words (their origin and the parts that comprise them). Most English words are derived from Latin, Greek, or Anglo-Saxon prefixes, suffixes, and roots. Thus, learning these bases may be the most flexible and simplest way to increase one's vocabulary. Each prefix, suffix, or root translates into a clue to the meaning of a word.

In the following pages you will find prefixes, suffixes, and roots, with one example of each. Learning a prefix, suffix, or root for one word will help you understand other words derived from the same base.

Prefixes and Word Roots

	Prefix/Root	Meaning	Example
1.	a	lacking	atheist: lacking belief in God
2.	a	to	abet: to aid
3.	ab	away	abduct: to lead away by force
4.	acantho	spiny	acanthus: a spiny herb
5.	acer	bitter	acerbic: bitter
6.	acid	bitter	acrid: bitter
7.	acous	hearing	acoustic: relating to hearing
8.	acri	bitter	acrimonious: bitterly quarrelsome
9.	acro	top	acropolis: a fortified height of a city
10.	act	do	activate: to make active
11.	ad	to	adjure: to command, to ask
12.	adeno	gland	adenoma: a benign tumor of glandular origin
13.	ag	act	agile: having quick motion
14.	agi	go	agile: quick
15.	ago	drive	agog: eager

	Prefix/Root	Meaning	Example
16.	agro	field	agronomy: the science of crop production
17.	ali	other	alias: a false name
18.	alt	high	altitude: a high location
19.	altr	other	altruism: living for others
20.	am	love	amatory: expressing love
21.	ambi	both	ambidextrous: able to use both hands
22.	ambul	walk	ambulant: able to walk
23.	amphi	two	amphibious: able to live on land and in water
24.	ana	up	anabasis: a journey upward
25.	andro	man	androgen: a male sex hormone
26.	anim	spirit	animated: elevated in spirit
27.	annu	year	annual: every year
28.	ante	before	antecedent: going before in time
29.	anthrop	man	anthropoid: resembling a man
30.	anti	against	antidote: a remedy against a poison

Prefixes and Word Roots

	Prefix/Root	Meaning	Example
1.	ap	toward	appease: to bring toward peace
2.	apo	away from	apostasy: a move away from a religious faith
3.	aqua	water	aquarium: a tank for fish
4.	arch	chief	archbishop: a chief bishop
5.	aud	hear	audible: able to be heard
6.	auto	self	autonomous: self-governing
7.	be	thoroughly	befuddle: to confuse thoroughly

	Prefix/Root	Meaning	Example
8.	belli	war	antebellum: existing before the war
9.	ben	good	benign: kind
10.	bene	good	benevolent: good-hearted
11.	bi	two	biennial: every two years
12.	biblio	book	bibliophile: a lover of books
13.	bio	life	biology: the science of life
14.	bon	good	bonhomie: good-heartedness
15.	brev	short	brevity: shortness
16.	bur	money	bursar: a treasurer
17.	caco	bad	cacophonous: bad sounding
18.	cad	fall	cascade: a waterfall
19.	calli	beautiful	calligraphy: beautiful handwriting
20.	calor	heat	caloric: giving off heat
21.	cant	sing	cantata: a musical composition
22.	cap	take	captivation: an effort to take something through flattery
23.	capit	head	capitation: a tax based on heads (individuals)
24.	cardio	heart	cardiology: the study of the heart
25.	carn	flesh	carnivorous: flesh eating
26.	cata	down	cataract: a waterfall
27.	ced	yield	concede: to yield
28.	cent	hundred	centipede: an insect with one hundred legs
29.	centr	center	centrifugal: to move away from the center
30.	cern	sift	discern: to discriminate

Prefixes and Word Roots

	Prefix/Root	Meaning	Example
1.	chrome	color	achromatic: without color
2.	chron	time	chronicle: an event in order of time
3.	cide	kill	homicide: the killing of one human by another human
4.	circ	around	circuitous: in a roundabout way
5.	cit	rouse	suscitate: to arouse
6.	clam	shout	declamation: a speech
7.	clast	destroy	iconoclast: one who destroys images
8.	clin	slope	incline: a slope
9.	cliv	slope	declivity: a downward slope
10.	clois	shut	cloister: to shut up
11.	clu	shut	occlude: to shut out
12.	cogn	know	cognizant: aware
13.	com	with	compunction: with regret
14.	con	with	concur: to agree with
15.	contra	against	contrary: opposed
16.	cord	heart	cordial: warmhearted
17.	corp	body	corporeal: pertaining to the body
18.	cosmo	world	cosmopolitan: belonging to all the world
19.	crac	rule	democracy: rule by the people
20.	cre	grow	accretion: growth in size
21.	cred	believe	credulous: believing easily
22.	cresc	grow	crescendo: growing in loudness
23.	culp	blame	culpable: deserving blame
24.	cumb	lean back	recumbent: leaning back
25.	cur	care for	curator: one who cares for a museum

	Prefix/Root	Meaning	Example
26.	curs	run	cursory: rapid
27.	de	down	declinate: having a downward slope
28.	dec	attractive	decorous: showing good taste
29.	dec	ten	decathlon: an athletic contest of ten events
30.	dem	people	epidemic: affecting many people

Prefixes and Word Roots

	Prefix/Root	Meaning	Example
1.	demn	harm	indemnity: to protect against harm (loss)
2.	denti	tooth	dentigerous: having teeth
3.	di	two	dichotomy: a division into two parts
4.	dia	through	dialectic: an argument through a discussion
5.	dict	say	maledictory: speaking evil of someone
6.	dign	worthy	dignify: to make worthy
7.	dis	away	dismiss: to send away
8.	dis	not	disaffected: not friendly
9.	dit	give	extradite: to give up a criminal from one state to another
10.	diurn	day	diurnal: daily
11.	doc	teach	docile: easily taught
12.	dol	pain	dolorous: painful
13.	domin	rule	dominion: a territory of rule
14.	dox	belief	orthodox: having to do with conventional beliefs
15.	duct	lead	abduct: to lead away by force (kidnap)

	Prefix/Root	Meaning	Example
16.	dur	lasting	perdurable: everlasting
17.	e, ex	out	exodus: the departure of the Israelites from Egypt
18.	ec	out of	eczema: a breaking out of the skin
19.	ef	out of	efflux: a flowing out
20.	ego	self	ego: self-esteem
21.	em	on	embark: to board a vessel for a trip
22.	empt	take	preempt: to take for oneself
23.	en	in	envenom: to put poison into
24.	entom	insect	entomology: the study of insects
25.	epi	among	epidemic: a spreading among a population
26.	epi	upon	epitaph: an inscription upon a gravestone
27.	err	wander	errant: wandering
28.	eu	good	euphoria: a good feeling
29.	ex	out of	expunge: to rub out
30.	extr	outward	extricate: to free

Prefixes and Word Roots

	Prefix/Root	Meaning	Example
1.	extra	beyond	extraneous: beyond that which is necessary
2.	fab	speak	ineffable: inexpressible
3.	fac	do	facient: a doer or agent
4.	fal	deceive	fallacious: deceptive
5.	fer	carry	pestiferous: carrying disease
6.	ferv	boil	effervescent: bubbling or vivacious
7.	fid	faith	diffident: lacking faith in oneself
8.	fig	shape	effigy: a representation of a person

	Prefix/Root	Meaning	Example
9.	fila	thread	filate: threadlike
10.	fin	limit	infinity: unlimited
11.	flag	fire	conflagrate: to burn up
12.	flam	fire	flambeau: a torch
13.	flex	bend	flexible: easily bent
14.	flor	flower	florid: flowery
15.	flu	flow	effluent: flowing out
16.	fore	previous	forefathers: ancestors
17.	form	shape	cuneiform: having the shape of a wedge
18.	fort	chance	fortuitous: occurring by chance
19.	fract	break	fractious: breaking rules
20.	fug	flee	fugacious: fleeting
21.	fulg	flash	fulgent: bright
22.	funct	perform	perfunctory: performed without care
23.	fus	pour	effuse: pouring out
24.	garrio	talk	garrulous: talkative
25.	gen	beget	progenitor: an ancestor
26.	gen	class	generic: of a general class
27.	gen	kind	genial: having a kind disposition
28.	geo	earth	geology: the study of the earth
29.	germ	vital part	germane: pertinent

Prefixes and Word Roots

	Prefix/Root	Meaning	Example
1.	gest	carry	gestate: to carry during pregnancy
2.	gnos	know	gnome: a wise saying
3.	grad	step	graduate: to pass from one stage to a higher one

	Prefix/Root	Meaning	Example
4.	graph	write	epigraph: an inscription on a monument
5.	grat	pleasing	grateful: pleasing
6.	greg	flock	aggregate: a collection
7.	gress	walk	gressorial: adapted for walking
8.	griev	heavy	grieve: heavy distress
9.	gyn	woman	misogyny: a hatred of women
10.	habit	have	habitat: a home
11.	hagio	holy	hagiography: a biography of a saint
12.	hap	by chance	hapless: unlucky
13.	helio	sun	heliocentric: regarding sun as center
14.	hemo	blood	hematic: having to do with blood
15.	hetero	other	heterosexual: attracted to the opposite sex
16.	hier	sacred	hierarchy: a ruling body of clergy
17.	hol	whole	catholic: universal
18.	homo	man	Homo sapiens: mankind
19.	homo	same	homogenize: to make uniform
20.	hosp	host	hospice: a home for the sick
21.	hume	earth	exhume: to unearth
22.	hydro	water	hydrophyte: a plant growing in water
23.	hyper	excessive	hyperbole: an exaggeration
24.	hypo	beneath	hypodermic: beneath the skin
25.	il	not	illicit: not legal
26.	im	not	implacable: not capable of forgiveness
27.	in	in	incarcerate: to put in jail

	Prefix/Root	Meaning	Example
28.	in	not	innocuous: not harmful
29.	int	within	intimate: closely acquainted
30.	inter	between	interlude: an intervening period of time

Prefixes and Word Roots

	Prefix/Root	Meaning	Example
1.	intra	within	intramural: within a single institution
2.	ir	not	irresolute: not resolute
3.	it	between	itinerant: traveling place to place
4.	jec	throw	projectile: an object thrown
5.	jour	day	sojourn: a temporary stay
6.	jud	judge	adjudicate: to judge
7.	junc	join	adjunct: something joined
8.	jur	swear	adjure: to command
9.	lat	carry	ablation: a carrying away
10.	lav	wash	lavabo: a ritual washing
11.	lect	choose	select: to choose
12.	leg	law	legal: according to law
13.	leg	read	legible: able to read
14.	lev	light	levity: a lack of seriousness
15.	lex	read	lexicon: a dictionary
16.	liber	free	libertine: a free thinker
17.	lig	bind	ligature: anything that binds
18.	ling	tongue	linguistics: relating to language
19.	liqu	liquid	deliquesce: to melt away
20.	lith	stone	monolith: a single stone
21.	loc	a place	locus: a place
22.	logo	word	logotype: a trademark

	Prefix/Root	Meaning	Example
23.	loq	speak	elocution: the art of public speaking
24.	lu	wash	ablution: a ceremonial washing
25.	luc	clear	elucidate: to make clear
26.	luc	light	translucent: transparent
27.	lud	deceive	delude: to deceive
28.	macro	large	macrocyte: a large red blood cell
29.	mag	great	magnanimous: great or noble
30.	magna	great	magnate: a great or important person

Prefixes and Word Roots

	Prefix/Root	Meaning	Example
1.	magni	great	magnitude: greatness
2.	magnus	big	magnanimous: generous or big in overlooking insult
3.	mal	bad	malign: to slander
4.	man	hand	manacles: handcuffs
5.	mater	mother	matrilineal: a descendent on the mother's side
6.	medi	middle	medieval: of the Middle Ages
7.	mega	great	megapod: having large feet
8.	mem	remember	memento: memorabilia
9.	ment	mind	dementia: a loss of mental abilities
10.	merc	trade	mercantile: pertaining to trade
11.	meta	beyond	metamorphosis: a change in form
12.	meter	measure	commensurate: having the same size or measure
13.	micro	small	microbe: a small organism causing disease
14.	mis	bad	miscreant: a bad person

	Prefix/Root	Meaning	Example
15.	miso	hate	misogynist: a hater of women
16.	miss	send	missive: a letter
17.	mit	send	transmit: to send
18.	mob	move	mobile: capable of moving
19.	mod	manner	mode: manner
20.	moll	soft	mollusk: an invertebrate with a soft body
21.	mon	warn	premonition: a forewarning
22.	mono	one	monolith: a statue made from a single block of stone
23.	mor	custom	mores: the customs of a group
24.	mor	death	mortuary: a funeral home
25.	mori	death	moribund: dying
26.	morph	shape	anthropomorphic: having human shape
27.	mot	move	motion: movement
28.	mov	move	remove: to take away
29.	multi	many	multitude: many
30.	mun	gift	munificent: generous

Prefixes and Word Roots

	Prefix/Root	Meaning	Example
1.	mut	change	immutable: not capable of changing
2.	nasc	born	nascent: being born
3.	nat	be born	prenatal: before birth
4.	nau	ship	nautical: pertaining to ships
5.	neg	deny	renege: to deny
6.	neo	new	neophyte: one who is new at something

	Prefix/Root	Meaning	Example
7.	nex	bind	nexus: a connection
8.	nic	harm	pernicious: harmful
9.	nihil	none	annihilation: the act of nullifying
10.	noc	hurt	innocuous: harmless
11.	nom	name	agnomen: a nickname
12.	non	not; no	nonentity: a person of no importance
13.	not	know	notorious: widely known unfavorably
14.	nov	new	novel: new
15.	nunc	announce	enunciate: to pronounce clearly
16.	ob	against	obdurate: resistant
17.	oc	against	occlude: to block out
18.	octa	eight	octad: a group of eight
19.	of	against	officious: intrusive
20.	omni	all	omniscient: all knowing
21.	omni	everywhere	omnipresent: present everywhere
22.	oner	burden	onerous: involving a burden
23.	oper	work	cooperate: to work with others
24.	ornitho	bird	ornithoid: resembling a bird
25.	ortho	straight	orthodox: conforming to established doctrines
26.	oss	bone	ossuary: a cemetery
27.	over	above	over: above
28.	pac	peace	pacific: peaceful
29.	palp	feel	palpable: able to be felt
30.	pan	all	panacea: a cure-all

Prefixes and Word Roots

	Prefix/Root	Meaning	Example
1.	par	equal	disparate: not alike
2.	para	beyond	paradox: a contradiction
3.	part	share	impart: to share
4.	pater	father	paternal: like a father
5.	path	disease	pathological: pertaining to disease
6.	path	feeling	apathy: a lack of feeling
7.	pec	money	impecunious: having no money
8.	ped	child	pediatrician: a medical doctor who treats children
9.	pel	drive	impel: to drive forward
10.	pen	almost	penumbra: a space of partial illumination
11.	pen	punish-ment	penance: a voluntary suffering
12.	pend	weight	impending: looming
13.	per	com-pletely	peremptory: complete authority
14.	peri	around	peripatetic: walking around
15.	pet	go	impetus: the driving force
16.	phan	show	diaphanous: see-through
17.	phil	love	philanthropic: the love of mankind
18.	phob	fear	xenophobia: the fear of strangers
19.	phone	sound	phonetics: study of speech sounds
20.	photo	light	photosphere: a sphere of light or radiance
21.	picro	bitter	picrotoxin: a bitter, poisonous solid
22.	pict	to paint	picture: a representation
23.	pla	please	implacable: incapable of pleasing
24.	ple	full	plenary: attended by all

	Prefix/Root	Meaning	Example
25.	pli	fold	explicate: to unfold the meaning or to make clear
26.	pod	foot	podiatrist: a foot doctor
27.	polit	city	cosmopolitan: a citizen of the world
28.	poly	many	polyglot: one who speaks many languages
29.	port	carry	portable: able to be carried
30.	post	after	posthumous: after death

Prefixes and Word Roots

	Prefix/Root	Meaning	Example
1.	pot	drink	potable: drinkable
2.	pot	powerful	plenipotentiary: having full power
3.	pre	before	precedent: something occurring before
4.	prec	pray	imprecate: to pray for misfortune
5.	preh	seize	apprehend: to seize
6.	press	press	oppress: to press against
7.	prim	early	primitive: of the earliest times
8.	pro	forth	prolific: bringing forth; being productive
9.	prob	prove	approbation: to approve
10.	prop	near	propinquity: nearness
11.	prop	one's own	proprietary: owned by
12.	proto	first	prototype: an original
13.	pseudo	false	pseudonym: a fictitious name used by an author
14.	psych	mind	psychology: the study of the mind
15.	pug	fight	pugilism: boxing
16.	puls	push	impulse: a sudden action

	Prefix/Root	Meaning	Example
17.	punc	point	punctuate: to mark with points
18.	pur	cleanse	purge: to cleanse away impurities
19.	put	think	putative: commonly thought
20.	pyro	fire	pyromania: a compulsion to set things on fire
21.	quad	four	quadrilateral: having four sides
22.	quer	ask	query: to ask
23.	ques	seek	quest: the act of seeking
24.	quie	quiet	quiescent: calm
25.	quint	five	quintuplets: five children born at one birth
26.	quir	ask	inquire: to ask
27.	rav	seize	ravish: to seize
28.	re	again	reiterate: to say again
29.	re	back	reimburse: to pay back
30.	rect	rule	rectitude: right conduct

Prefixes and Word Roots

	Prefix/Root	Meaning	Example
1.	reg	rule	regent: a ruler
2.	retro	backward	retrograde: moving backward
3.	rhino	nose	rhinoplasty: plastic surgery of the nose
4.	rid	laugh	deride: to laugh at
5.	ris	laugh	risible: laughable
6.	roga	ask	interrogate: to question
7.	rud	crude	erudite: not crude; learned
8.	rupt	to break	erupt: to break through
9.	sacr	holy	sacrosanct: holy
10.	sal	healthy	salubrious: healthful

	Prefix/Root	Meaning	Example
11.	sanct	holy	sanctimonious: holy
12.	sangui	blood	consanguinity: relationship by blood
13.	sap	taste	sapient: having good taste
14.	sapro	decompose	saprophyte: an organism that lives on dead organic matter
15.	sat	enough	insatiable: never enough
16.	sci	know	prescience: foreknowledge
17.	scrib	write	inscribe: to write as a lasting record
18.	se	aside	sequester: to separate or set aside
19.	sed	sit	sedentary: staying in one place
20.	sem	seed	seminal: relating to seed
21.	semi	half	semiannual: half of a year
22.	sen	old	senesce: to grow old
23.	sent	feel	sentient: able to feel or perceive
24.	seq	follow	sequacious: following with regularity
25.	serv	serve	servile: slavelike
26.	sign	sign	signet: a sign
27.	sim	resembling	similitude: resemblance
28.	sin	curve	sinuous: curving
29.	sip	taste	insipid: tasteless; dull
30.	soci	companion	associate: a companion

Prefixes and Word Roots

	Prefix/Root	Meaning	Example
1.	sol	alone	solo: alone
2.	sol	sun	solarium: a sunning place
3.	solv	solve	resolute: determined to solve a problem

	Prefix/Root	Meaning	Example
4.	somn	sleep	somnambulism: sleepwalking
5.	son	sound	consonance: a pleasing sound
6.	soph	wisdom	sophomoric: not wise; immature
7.	spec	look	specious: looking genuine but not
8.	spir	breathe	inspire: to breathe in
9.	sta	stand	stanchion: an upright stand
10.	steno	short	stenograph: to write in shorthand
11.	stri	bind	stringent: strict
12.	struct	build	construct: to build
13.	suad	sway	assuage: to lessen distress
14.	sub	under	subjugate: to bring under control
15.	suc	beneath	succumb: to submit
16.	sult	leap	desultory: leaping from topic to topic
17.	summ	highest	consummate: of the highest degree
18.	super	beyond	superfluous: beyond what is necessary
19.	sur	more	surtax: more (an additional) tax
20.	surge	rise	resurgence: a rising again to prominence
21.	sym	together	symbiotic: mutually together for benefit
22.	syn	together	syndicate: together for business purposes
23.	tacit	silent	taciturn: disinclined to talk
24.	tact	touch	tactile: perceptible by touch
25.	tain	hold	maintain: to hold in an existing state
26.	tang	touch	tangible: able to be touched or understood
27.	tele	across	telecast: to transmit across a distance

	Prefix/Root	Meaning	Example
28.	tele	far	telephone: literally, "a voice from afar"
29.	temp	temper	temperance: moderation in behavior
30.	ten	belong to	appurtenant: belonging to

Prefixes and Word Roots

	Prefix/Root	Meaning	Example
1.	ten	hold	tenable: capable of being held or defended
2.	tens	stretch	tensile: able to be stretched
3.	term	end	terminate: to end
4.	terr	earth	extraterrestrial: not from earth
5.	test	witness	attest: to witness as true
6.	therm	heat	thermometer: a device to measure the temperature
7.	thermo	heat	thermodynamic: using or producing heat
8.	tim	fear	timorous: fearful
9.	topo	place	topography: a detailed mapping of an area
10.	tort	twist	contort: to twist
11.	tract	pull	intractable: unmanageable
12.	trans	over	transcend: to cross over to a higher level
13.	trep	shake	trepidation: apprehension
14.	tri	three	trilogy: three literary works in a series
15.	trud	thrust	detrude: to thrust down
16.	tur	turmoil	perturbed: disorderly
17.	ultra	beyond	ultraviolet: beyond the limit of visibility

	Prefix/Root	Meaning	Example
18.	umbr	shadow	adumbrate: to overshadow
19.	un	not	unbelievable: not believable
20.	und	wave	undulate: to move up and down
21.	uni	one	unicycle: a vehicle with a single wheel
22.	urb	city	urbane: civilized
23.	vac	empty	vacant: empty
24.	vag	wandering	vagrant: one who wanders

Prefixes and Word Roots

	Prefix/Root	Meaning	Example
1.	val	farewell	valedictory address: a farewell address
2.	val	valor	valor: bravery
3.	ven	come	convene: to come together
4.	ver	true	veracious: truthful
5.	verb	word	verbose: wordy
6.	vert	turn	avert: to turn from
7.	via	way	viaduct: an arched roadway
8.	vic	substitute	vicarious: substitutionary
9.	vid	see	video: a visual picture
10.	vil	mean	vile: evil
11.	vinc	conquer	evincible: able to be conquered
12.	vind	avenge	vindicate: to clear from blame
13.	vis	see	vista: a view from a distance
14.	viv	life	vivacious: lively
15.	voc	call	avocation: a hobby or minor calling
16.	vok	call	convoke: to call together
17.	vol	wish	malevolent: ill wishing

	Prefix/Root	Meaning	Example
18.	voro	eating	omnivorous: eating any food
19.	vow	voice	avow: to voice openly
20.	vuls	tear out	divulsion: tearing apart
21.	with	away	withdraw: to take away

Suffixes

	Suffix	Meaning	Example
1.	able	able	bearable: able to endure
2.	acy	state	bankruptcy: the state of having no money
3.	ade	action	fusillade: a rapid discharge of firearms
4.	age	act of	pillage: an act of robbery
5.	al	relating to	reprisal: paying back evil for evil
6.	algia	pain	neuralgia: sharp pain along a nerve
7.	an	one who	artisan: one who makes crafts
8.	ance	state	affiance: the state of being joined together
9.	arch	rule	monarch: a ruler
10.	ard	one that does excessively	drunkard: one who drinks to excess
11.	asis	action	anabasis: a military action or advance
12.	ate	make	attenuate: to make thin
13.	ation	state	starvation: the state of being starved
14.	chrome	color	monochrome: a painting in different shades of one color
15.	cian	having a certain skill	pyrotechnician: an expert at displaying fireworks
16.	cit	set in motion	incite: to move to action

	Suffix	Meaning	Example
17.	crat	rule	autocrat: a ruler holding unlimited powers
18.	cumb	lie down	recumbent: lying down
19.	cy	condition	accuracy: the condition of correctness
20.	dom	state	wisdom: the state of being wise
21.	ee	one who receives the action	collatee: one on whom the income of a church office is bestowed
22.	en	made of	molten: made by melting
23.	en	cause to be	deepen: to cause to become deeper
24.	ence	quality	opulence: the quality of plenty; wealth
25.	ency	quality	belligerency: the quality of having a fighting spirit
26.	er	one who	jester: one who tells jokes
27.	esis	process	exegesis: the process of interpretation of Scripture

Suffixes

	Suffix	Meaning	Example
1.	esque	like	picturesque: like a picture
2.	ess	feminine	lioness: a female lion
3.	ferous	bearing	auriferous: bearing gold
4.	fic	making	beatific: making blessed
5.	ful	full of	vengeful: full of plans to repay evil for evil
6.	fy	make	vitrify: to make into glass
7.	gnosis	knowledge	prognosis: a forecast of the probable course of a disease
8.	gon	angle	hexagon: a polygon having six angles and six sides

	Suffix	Meaning	Example
9.	hood	state of	manhood: the state of being a man
10.	ible	able	edible: able to be eaten
11.	ic	like	metaphoric: like a metaphor, a figure of speech
12.	ile	suited for	docile: suited for being taught
13.	ine	nature of	saccharine: of the nature of sugar
14.	ion	state	union: the state of being joined
15.	ish	resembling	boorish: resembling a rude person
16.	ish	suggesting	churlish: suggesting a rude, ill-bred person
17.	ism	practice	socialism: a practice of all members of a society sharing in products
18.	ism	manner	colloquialism: an informal manner of speech
19.	ist	one who	cellist: one who is an artist with the cello
20.	ition	action	sedition: an action of treason
21.	itis	inflammation	appendicitis: an inflammation of the appendix
22.	ity	state	civility: the state of being polite
23.	ity	quality	celerity: the quality of quickness
24.	ive	causing	deliberative: tending to be careful
25.	ize	make	pauperize: to make poor
26.	less	without	hapless: without luck

Suffixes

	Suffix	Meaning	Example
1.	like	like	childlike: like a child
2.	logue	type of speaking or writing	prologue: an introduction to a play or poem

	Suffix	Meaning	Example
3.	ly	like	listlessly: like one who is without spirit
4.	mania	craving	bibliomania: excessive craving of books
5.	ment	state of	aggrandizement: the state of becoming greater
6.	ness	state of	artlessness: the state of being without guile
7.	ology	study	etymology: the study of words
8.	opia	sight	myopia: nearsightedness
9.	or	office	juror: a member of a jury
10.	osis	condition	neurosis: a nervous condition
11.	ous	full of	opprobrious: full of reproach
12.	pathy	suffering	sympathy: the ability to share the sufferings of another
13.	phone	sound	megaphone: a device for magnifying sound
14.	phyte	plant	lithophyte: a plant growing on rocks
15.	plasm	matter	protoplasm: the living matter of cells
16.	ship	office	chancellorship: the office of the head of a university
17.	some	showing	lonesome: showing loneliness
18.	th	state	warmth: the state of being warm
19.	tomy	cutting	dichotomy: a difference of opinion
20.	tude	condition of	verisimilitude: the condition of being similar
21.	ty	state	enmity: the state of hostility
22.	ure	state of	censure: the state of finding fault with
23.	voc	call	convoke: to call a meeting

	Suffix	Meaning	Example
24.	ward	in the direction of	homeward: in the direction of home
25.	y	tends to	wary: tends to be watchful

11

Abbreviations, Symbols, and Equations

$$E = mc^2$$

Albert Einstein
1879–1955

Ask almost anyone on the street to name a brilliant person of history and he or she will say, "Einstein." In 1905 he gave us the theory of relativity, $E = mc^2$. E stands for *energy*, m stands for *mass*, and c^2 stands for *the speed of light squared*. No library could possibly contain the subsequent books on Einstein's famous equation, and the implications of his equation boggle our minds even today. Think about this: if we traveled at the speed of light into space, would we really be the same age when we returned as when we started?

All the scientific mystery aside, here is the pertinent question for us in our challenge to increase our mental capacity:

What made Einstein so brilliant? He was not a child prodigy, but he was smart and given to independent study. As a youth he loved the work of the musical genius Mozart, so Einstein taught himself to play the piano. He enjoyed Latin as well as mathematics and taught himself algebra at age twelve. In graduate school he taught himself electricity and magnetism.

The applications for us from Einstein are significant. We need knowledge of words in several fields to develop brilliance. We need to commit to independent study in order to improve our intellect. And a little knowledge of Latin words won't hurt either.

Often, synonyms are created by abbreviating a word or phrase. More and more our society, and our dictionaries, recognize abbreviations as actual words. Learning appropriate abbreviations and their meanings will increase your ability to read and understand.

Also included in this chapter are terms used for various units of measure. Learning these will help you not only in reading comprehension but also in many practical areas of your life.

Abbreviations, Symbols, and Measures

1. @: at
2. ∞: infinity
3. π: pi (3.1416)
4. AAA: American Automobile Association
5. ABC: American Broadcasting Corporation
6. ac: before meals
7. AC: alternating current
8. ACT: American College Test
9. AD: in the year of our Lord
10. Ag: silver
11. aka: also known as
12. a.m.: in the morning

13. AMA: American Medical Association

14. anon.: anonymous

15. approx.: approximately

16. As: arsenic

17. ASAP: as soon as possible

18. atty.: attorney

19. Au: gold

20. AV: audiovisual

21. BA: Bachelor of Arts degree

22. BBB: Better Business Bureau

23. BC: before Christ

24. BCE: before the Common Era

25. bid: twice daily

26. BS: Bachelor of Science degree

27. C: carbon

28. Ca: calcium

29. CEO: chief executive officer

30. CIA: Central Intelligence Agency

31. Cl: chlorine

32. Cr: chromium

33. Cu: copper

34. DD: Doctor of Divinity degree

35. DDS: Doctor of Dental Science

36. DNA: deoxyribonucleic acid

37. d.t.'s: delirium tremens

38. DUI: driving under the influence

39. e.g.: for example

40. $E = mc^2$: energy equals mass times the speed of light squared

Abbreviations and Measures

1. et al.: and others

2. etc.: and so on

3. f: forte (loud sound in music)

4. FDA: Food and Drug Administration

5. Fe: Iron

6. G: giga- (1,000,000,000)
7. H: hydrogen
8. He: helium
9. Hx: history
10. I: iodine
11. ibid.: in the same place
12. i.e.: that is
13. IQ: intelligence quotient
14. JD: Doctor of Law degree
15. K: potassium
16. lb.: pound
17. LLD: Doctor of Law degree
18. Mg: magnesium
19. mg: milligram
20. N: nitrogen
21. Na: sodium
22. Ni: nickel
23. O: oxygen
24. oz.: ounce
25. P: phosphorus
26. Pb: lead
27. pc: after meals
28. PhD: Doctor of Philosophy degree
29. p.m.: after noon
30. prn: as needed
31. pro tem: for the time being
32. PS: postscript
33. QED: which was to be demonstrated
34. Ra: radium
35. S: sulfur
36. Sn: tin
37. tid: three times daily
38. U: uranium
39. UK: United Kingdom
40. Z: zinc

Unit-of-Measure Words

The words below are various measurements.

1. bolt: cloth
2. calorie: heat
3. caliber: bullet
4. joule: energy

5. karat: weight (jeweler's measure)
6. newton: force
7. cord: logs
8. meter: length
9. elite: type
10. gauge: interior diameter of the barrel of a shotgun
11. pica: type
12. watt: electrical power
13. fathom: water depth
14. hectares: land surface area
15. knot: speed on the sea
16. league: water depth
17. volts: the force of an electric current
18. Beaufort scale: wind forces
19. Richter scale: earthquakes
20. pH scale: acid or base—0 is an acid, 14 is a base, 7 is neutral

12

Foreign Words

We urge you, brethren, admonish the unruly, encourage
the fainthearted, help the weak, be patient with everyone.

1 Thessalonians 5:14 (NASB)

In the original Greek language of the New Testament, five
Greek verbs were used in this passage to the Thessalonians
to describe five variations of counseling: *parakaleo, noutheteo, paramutheomai, antechomai,* and *makrothumeo. Parakaleo*
means "to exhort, beseech, encourage, or comfort." *Noutheteo*
means "to warn, to confront." *Paramutheomai* means "to cheer
up, to encourage." *Antechomai* means "to hold up, to support."
Makrothumeo means "to be patient."

While the above words in their original language may lie
beyond the grasp of people with no formal training in Greek,
they illustrate a good principle: many thousands of foreign
words that were once known by few have slowly amalgamated

their way into the English language. In fact, nouthetic (from *noutheteo* above) counseling became popular several years ago in books by Jay Adams, and now it is widely assimilated into the language of most Christian counselors.

Foreign words start as foreign, then become "double agents" and are used in both the foreign and the English languages, and eventually are fully incorporated into the English language. Lexicographer John McWhorter believes that 99 percent of English words are derived from other languages. The following words are double agents from various languages such as French, Greek, Latin, Italian, Spanish, German, Yiddish, and Japanese.

Foreign Words

1. amicus curiae: a friend of the court
2. idée fixe: a fixed idea
3. hoi polloi: the masses
4. milieu: an environment
5. quixotic: imaginary
6. raconteur: a person skilled in relating anecdotes
7. soupçon: a hint
8. savoir faire: a knowledge of what to say
9. décolletage: the neckline of a dress
10. qui vive: to be on the alert
11. quid pro quo: one thing for another
12. de facto: in fact
13. postprandial: after dinner
14. parvenu: an upstart in wealth
15. gemütlich: agreeable
16. par excellence: excellence
17. leitmotiv: a recurring musical theme

18. avant-garde: new
19. bête noire: something feared
20. bon mot: witticism
21. gauche: lacking grace
22. aficionado: a devotee
23. peccadillo: a minor offense
24. garrote: to strangle
25. presidio: a garrison
26. ersatz: a fake
27. tout à fait: entirely
28. angst: anxiety
29. Götterdämmerung: total destruction
30. echt: authentic
31. kaput: ruined
32. tout de suite: immediately
33. ganef: a thief
34. tout le monde: everyone
35. klutz: an awkward person
36. kvell: delighted
37. addendum: a list of additions
38. mensch: an admirable person
39. nebbish: a timid person
40. nosh: a snack
41. nudge: to pester
42. impresario: a manager
43. schnook: a pathetic person
44. tsuris: worries
45. incognito: having one's identity concealed
46. yenta: a busybody
47. anomie: alienation
48. diatribe: a denunciation
49. plethora: a great number
50. psyche: the human soul
51. dolor: sorrow
52. exemplar: a model
53. decorum: dignified behavior
54. exigent: urgent
55. prolix: wordy

56. sanctum: the holiest of places
57. terra incognita: unknown territory
58. sub rosa: secretly
59. status quo: the existing state
60. sotto voce: a low, soft voice

Foreign Words

1. alfresco: outdoors
2. imbroglio: a difficult situation
3. inamorata: a female sweetheart
4. incognito: having one's identity concealed
5. in toto: in the whole
6. maestro: an eminent composer
7. vendetta: a bitter feud
8. virtuoso: a skilled performer
9. prima donna: a vain person
10. caudillo: a head of state
11. envoy: a diplomatic agent
12. esprit de corps: a sense of union
13. laissez-faire: a policy of noninterference
14. milieu: an environment
15. repartee: a quick reply
16. riposte: a quick retort
17. tour de force: an exceptional achievement
18. au courant: up-to-date
19. adagio: slowly
20. carte blanche: full authority
21. coup de grace: a final blow
22. divertissement: entertainment
23. aficionado: a devotee
24. doyen: a leader in a field

25. éclat: flair

26. amor vincitomnia: love conquers all

27. élan: vivacity

28. ennui: boredom

29. ingenue: an innocent young woman

30. anno Domini: in the year of the Lord

31. mélange: a mixture

32. mot juste: the right word

33. ad locum: at the place

34. beau geste: a noble gesture

35. ad interim: in the meantime

36. blitzkrieg: a lightning war

37. ad valorem: in proportion to the value

38. ipso facto: by the fact itself

39. bon marché: inexpensive

40. modus operandi: a method of doing something

41. decessit sine prole: died without children

42. nota bene: to mark well

43. bonne chance: good luck

44. officio: by virtue of the office

45. persona non grata: an unwelcome person

46. pro tem: temporarily

47. pan passu: at an equal place

48. sine anno: without a date

49. quid pro quo: one thing for another

50. carpe diem: seize the opportunity

51. tovarish: a comrade

52. tempus fugit: time flies

53. amour propre: self-esteem

54. comme il faut: proper

55. dolce far niente: sweet idleness

56. de jure: by law

57. de rigueur: necessary

13

Specialized Fields: From Christianity to Physics

Just as I
have come from afar, creating pain for many—
men and women across the good green earth—
so let his name be Odysseus . . .
the Son of Pain, a name he'll earn in full.

Homer
c. 900–850 BC

Homer's *The Odyssey* is one of the earliest Greek works to survive to this day. This epic work is about the Trojan War and gives us our word *odyssey*, which means "a long and difficult journey." Many literary scholars consider Homer one of the most influential of all poets. Of course, his original work was long ago translated from Greek into English. However, like the word *odyssey*, many Greek words live on today: *alpha* ("the beginning"), *omega* ("the end"), *anathema* ("a loathed person"), *catharsis* ("a release of emotions"), *despot* ("a tyrant"), and *enigma* ("a riddle"), to name a few.

Ironically, a key to brilliance is often found in knowledge of Latin and Greek, the "dead" languages. They are often used in specific fields of knowledge or form root words that are spelled similar to the original word.

Specific Fields

A knowledge of specific fields is advantageous when relating to the broad array of people one may encounter on life's journey. The following words relate to the fields of theology, English, literature, music, art, math, and science, and are more specific and esoteric; they are for a brilliant mind.

Due to the nature of these fields, some of the definitions are longer than those in previous lists. However, staying with the challenge will assure you of not only a broader vocabulary but also a wider array of knowledge and topics. You may even discover a new interest or passion.

Incidentally, one can have cultural literacy and still eschew material that goes against one's personal values and convictions. I would advise against using any material in any field that is morally, spiritually, or philosophically objectionable.

Words from Christianity

1. grace: God's unmerited favor
2. faith: trust
3. righteousness: being just

4. propitiate: to appease
5. justify: to announce a favorable verdict
6. reconciliation: the doing away of enmity
7. redemption: deliverance by payment of a price
8. salvation: deliverance
9. depravity: humankind's innate wickedness
10. disciple: a pupil
11. exegesis: the explanation of a text
12. gift: a present
13. omnipotent: all-powerful
14. omnipresent: everywhere present
15. omniscient: all-knowing
16. repentance: a change of mind
17. vicarious: substitutionary
18. eschatology: the study of end times
19. epistemology: the study of the limits of knowledge
20. immutable: unchangeable
21. confess: to declare
22. justification: the act of God whereby humans are free from guilt
23. decalogue: the Ten Commandments
24. apostle: a messenger of Christ
25. monotheism: the belief in one God
26. Pentateuch: the first five books of the Bible
27. Sheol: the abode of the dead
28. Messiah: anointed one; a name for Christ
29. orthodox: conforming to established doctrines

30. heterodox: opposed to established doctrines
31. Assyria: modern-day Syria
32. Babylonia: modern-day Iraq
33. Persia: modern-day Iran
34. homiletics: the art of preparing sermons
35. Passion: the suffering of Jesus
36. vicarious atonement: substitutionary reconciliation

Words from English

1. noun: a part of speech that names a person, place, or thing; one of the two elements of a sentence
2. verb: a part of speech that indicates an action; one of the two elements of a sentence
3. gerund: a verb functioning as a noun; the -ing form of a verb, such as *speaking*
4. pronoun: a word that replaces a noun
5. tense: a form taken by a verb to indicate the time of action, such as present, past, future, present perfect, past perfect, and future perfect
6. infinitive: the base form of a verb, usually preceded by the preposition *to*
7. indicative mood: a verb form that makes a statement
8. imperative mood: a verb form that expresses a command
9. subjective mood: a verb form that uses a "that" clause
10. adjective: a part of speech that modifies a noun

11. adverb: a part of speech that modifies a verb, an adjective, or another adverb

12. preposition: a part of speech that connects, such as *at*, *through, by, on, across, for, like, with*, and *to*

13. prepositional phrase: a group of connected words containing a preposition but without a subject or verb

14. clause: a distinct part of a sentence that has a subject and a verb

15. conjunctions: joining words that link parts of sentences, such as *and, or,* and *but*

16. modifier: a word that adds information to other parts of a sentence

17. interrogative: having the form of a question

18. imperative: denoting a command

19. indicative: denoting statement of a fact

20. antecedent: the word to which a pronoun refers

Words from Literature

1. allegory: a poem or prose in which people or events are symbolic of actual events

2. alliteration: the repetition of initial consonant sounds

3. anagram: a word formed from the transposition of letters of another word

4. anaphora: the repetition of a phrase

5. annotation: explanatory notes

6. assonance: the repetition of vowel sounds

7. free verse: poetry without regular meter

8. canto: a major division of a long poem

9. consonance: the repetition of consonant sounds

10. couplet: two successive rhyming lines of poetry

11. epic: a long narrative poem

12. epistolary novel: a novel in letter form

13. genre: a classification of literary work

14. haiku: Japanese poetry made of three unrhymed lines

15. sonnet: a fourteen-line poem with a rigid rhyme scheme

16. motif: the recurring theme in a literary work

17. ode: a lyric poem

18. onomatopoeia: a word formed from its sound

19. oxymoron: an expression using two opposing terms

20. parable: a story that illustrates a moral truth

21. parody: a humorous literary work

22. personification: a figure of speech that gives human forms to abstractions

23. satire: a type of literary work that uses sarcasm

24. simile: a figure of speech making a comparison using *like* or *as*

25. metaphor: a figure of speech in which a statement of identity is made

26. metonymy: the use of the name of one object for another

27. paraleipsis: the deliberate, concise treatment of a topic to emphasize it

28. litotes: ironical understatement

29. panegyric: a eulogy
30. synecdoche: a figure of speech in which a part is used for the whole

Words from Literature: Authors and Their Works

1. Aeschylus: *Prometheus Bound*
2. Aesop: *The Boy Who Cried Wolf*
3. Anderson: *The Ugly Duckling*
4. Aristophanes: *The Frogs*
5. Aristotle: *Poetics*
6. Austen: *Pride and Prejudice*
7. Baldwin: *Go Tell It on the Mountain*
8. Balzac: *The Human Comedy*
9. Barrie: *Peter Pan*
10. Beckett: *Molloy*
11. Beyle (Stendhal): *The Red and the Black*
12. Blake: *Songs of Innocence*
13. Brontë: *Wuthering Heights*
14. Bryant: *Thanatopsis*
15. Buck: *The Good Earth*
16. Bunyan: *Pilgrim's Progress*
17. Burroughs: *Tarzan*
18. Carroll: *Alice in Wonderland*
19. Cather: *O Pioneers!*
20. Cervantes: *Don Quixote*
21. Chaucer: *The Canterbury Tales*
22. Chekhov: *The Cherry Orchard*
23. Clemens (Twain): *Tom Sawyer*
24. Conrad: *Lord Jim*
25. Cooper: *Leather-Stocking Tales*

26. Crane: *The Red Badge of Courage*
27. Dante: *The Divine Comedy*
28. Defoe: *Robinson Crusoe*
29. Dickens: *A Christmas Carol*
30. Dickinson: "Because I Could Not Stop for Death"
31. Donne: "The Flea"
32. Dostoyevsky: *Crime and Punishment*
33. Doyle: *Sherlock Holmes*
34. Dreiser: *Sister Carrie*
35. Dumas: *The Three Musketeers*

Words from Literature: Authors and Their Works

1. George Eliot: *Silas Marner*
2. T. S. Eliot: *Prufrock and Other Observations*
3. Emerson: *Concord Hymn*
4. Euripedes: *Medea*
5. Faulkner: *The Sound and the Fury*
6. Fitzgerald: *The Great Gatsby*
7. Forster: *A Passage to India*
8. Frost: "Stopping by Woods on a Snowy Evening"
9. Gardner: *Perry Mason*
10. Golding: *Lord of the Flies*
11. Hardy: *Far from the Madding Crowd*
12. Hawthorne: *The House of the Seven Gables*
13. Hemingway: *A Farewell to Arms*
14. Hersey: *A Bell for Adano*
15. Hesse: *Siddhartha*
16. Hilton: *Lost Horizon*
17. Homer: *The Iliad; The Odyssey*

18. Hugo: *The Hunchback of Notre Dame*
19. Huxley: *Brave New World*
20. Ibsen: *A Doll's House*
21. Irving: *Rip Van Winkle*
22. James: *Washington Square*
23. Johnson: *Dictionary of the English Language*
24. Jonson: *The Alchemist*
25. Joyce: *Ulysses*
26. Kafka: *The Metamorphosis*
27. Keats: "Ode to a Nightingale"
28. Kipling: *The Jungle Book*
29. Lewis: *Elmer Gantry*
30. London: *The Call of the Wild*
31. Longfellow: *Hiawatha*
32. Machiavelli: *The Prince*
33. Mann: *Death in Venice*
34. Marlowe: *The Jew of Malta*
35. Melville: *Moby Dick*

Words from Literature: Authors and Their Works

1. Miller: *Death of a Salesman*
2. Milne: *Winnie-the-Pooh*
3. Milton: *Paradise Lost*
4. Mitchell: *Gone with the Wind*
5. Morrison: *Song of Solomon*
6. Nabokov: *Invitation to a Beheading*
7. O'Neill: *The Iceman Cometh*
8. Orwell: *1984*
9. Paine: *Common Sense*
10. Petrarch: *Canzoniere*
11. Poe: "The Raven"
12. Pope: *An Essay on Man*
13. Proust: *Remembrance of Things Past*
14. Pushkin: *Eugene Onegin*

15. Remarque: *All Quiet on the Western Front*
16. Salinger: *The Catcher in the Rye*
17. Sandburg: *Chicago*
18. Scott: *Ivanhoe*
19. Shakespeare: *Romeo and Juliet*
20. Shaw: *Pygmalion*
21. Shelley: *Prometheus Unbound*
22. Sinclair: *The Jungle*
23. Sophocles: *Oedipus the King*
24. Steinbeck: *The Grapes of Wrath*
25. Stevenson: *Treasure Island*
26. Swift: *Gulliver's Travels*
27. Thoreau: *Walden*
28. Tolstoy: *War and Peace*
29. Verne: *Around the World in Eighty Days*
30. Virgil: *The Aeneid*
31. Walker: *The Color Purple*
32. White: *Charlotte's Web*
33. Whitman: *Leaves of Grass*
34. Wilder: *Our Town*
35. Williams: *The Glass Menagerie*
36. Wolfe: *You Can't Go Home Again*
37. Wordsworth: "The Daffodils"

Words from Music

1. adagio: a slow movement
2. allegro: a rather fast movement
3. alto: a lower female voice
4. andante: a moderate tempo
5. ballad: a folk song that tells a story
6. cantata: an extended choral work

7. chamber music: music intended for a room

8. chorale: a traditional hymn for congregational use

9. chord: a blending of two or more notes

10. coda: the final passage in a music movement

11. concerto: a composition for a solo instrument plus an orchestra

12. crescendo: music that gradually becomes louder

13. forte: loud music

14. largo: a very slow speed

15. legato: music without a break

16. libretto: the text of an opera

17. opera: a drama in which the characters sing

18. ostinato: music repeated

19. piano: soft music

20. presto: fast music

21. rondo: a composition in which one section recurs

22. sforzando: music with force

23. sonata: a musical composition in three or four movements

24. soprano: the highest female voice

25. symphony: an orchestral work in four movements

26. tenor: the highest male voice

27. tutti: music for full orchestra

28. vivace: lively music

Words from Music: Musicians and Their Works

1. Armstrong: *Hello, Dolly!*

2. Bach: *Brandenburg Concertos*

3. Bartók: *Bluebeard's Castle*

4. Bassie: "One O'Clock Jump"

5. Beethoven: *The Ninth Symphony*

6. Berlin: *White Christmas*

7. Berlioz: *Fantastic Symphony*

8. Bernstein: *West Side Story*

9. Borodin: *Prince Igor*

10. Brahms: *First, Second, Third,* and *Fourth Symphonies*

11. Chopin: *Études*

12. Cohan: *Yankee Doodle Dandy*

13. Copland: *The Tender Land*

14. Debussy: *Pelléas and Mélisande*

15. Dvořák: *From the New World*

16. Ellington: "Satin Doll"

17. Foster: "My Old Kentucky Home"

18. Gershwin: *An American in Paris*

19. Guthrie: "This Land Is Your Land"

20. Handel: *Messiah*

21. Haydn: *The Creation*

22. Ives: *Decoration Day*

23. Kodaly: *Psalmus hungaricus*

24. Liszt: *The Preludes*

25. Mahler: *Symphony of a Thousand*

26. Mendelssohn: *Elijah*

27. Milhaud: *Creation of the World*

28. Miller: *Moonlight Serenade*

29. Mozart: *The Marriage of Figaro*

30. Mussorgsky: *Night on Bald Mountain*

Words from Music: Musicians and Their Works

1. Orff: *Oedipus the Tyrant*

2. Paganini: *Bell Rondo*

3. Prokofiev: *Peter and the Wolf*
4. Puccini: *Madam Butterfly*
5. Rachmaninoff: *Rhapsody on a Theme of Paganini*
6. Rameau: *Castor and Pollux*
7. Ravel: *Spanish Rhapsody*
8. Rodgers: *The Sound of Music*
9. Rossini: *William Tell*
10. Schoenberg: *Moses and Aaron*
11. Schubert: *Impromptus*
12. Schumann: "The Happy Farmer"
13. Smetana: *The Bartered Bride*
14. Sousa: "The Stars and Stripes Forever"
15. Strauss: *Tales from the Vienna Woods*
16. Stravinsky: *The Firebird*
17. Tchaikovsky: *Sleeping Beauty*
18. Verdi: *Rigoletto*
19. Vivaldi: *The Four Seasons*
20. Wagner: *The Flying Dutchman*
21. Weil: *The Threepenny Opera*

Words from Art

1. abstract: emphasizes concept rather than physical reality
2. annunciation: the announcing of the incarnation by Gabriel
3. chiaroscuro: a light/dark technique
4. classicism: art from Greek and Rome; emphasizes harmony
5. cloisonné: a process of enameling with channels or cloisons

6. collage: a picture built from various materials
7. dada: bizarre works
8. fresco: a wall painting
9. frieze: the middle section of a building for a relief sculpture
10. gesso: a plaster and glue mixture
11. glazing: a process of applying transparent oil paint
12. impasto: the application of thick pigment to canvas
13. intaglio: a concave effect on an engraving
14. lithography: a method of printing
15. luminism: art associated with impressionism
16. mobile: a kinetic sculpture made of different materials hung at different levels
17. montage: one layer over another
18. naturalistic: realistic imitation
19. opaque: not transmitting light
20. pastiche: a piece of art similar to a previous one
21. primary colors: blue, red, and yellow
22. relief: a sculpture not free standing; a background
23. secondary colors: violet, orange, and green
24. serial art: the repetition of an image
25. serigraphy: a silk-screen painting
26. sfumato: a painting technique in which tones are blended
27. still life: inanimate objects
28. triptych: three panels
29. vignette: a decoration of leaves around the first letter of a chapter of a book

30. warp: vertical fibers
31. weft: horizontal fibers

Words from Art: Artists and Their Works

1. Adams: "Aspens"
2. Audubon: *Birds of America*
3. Bacon: Lincoln Memorial
4. Botticelli: *St. Sebastian*
5. Breuer: Whitney Museum of American Art
6. Brueghel: *The Hunters in the Snow*
7. Caldecott: illustrations in children's books
8. Calder: mobiles
9. Caravaggio: *The Conversion of St. Paul*
10. Cassatt: *Mother and Child*
11. Cellini: *Perseus* (bronze)
12. Cézanne: *The Black Clock*
13. Chagall: *The Juggler*
14. Cole: *Hudson River School*
15. Constable: *The Hay Wain*
16. Dalí: *The Persistence of Memory*
17. David: *The Death of Socrates*
18. da Vinci: *The Last Supper; Mona Lisa*
19. Durer: *Melancholia I*
20. El Greco: *The Annunciation*
21. Ernst: *Europe After the Rain*
22. Gainsborough: *The Blue Boy*
23. Giotto: *St. John the Baptist*
24. Gropius: Bauhaus architecture
25. Hogarth: *Signing the Marriage Contract*

26. Holbein: *The Dance of Death*
27. Homer: *Breaking Storm*
28. Johns: *Three Flags*
29. Matisse: *Fruits and Flowers*

Words from Art: Artists and Their Works

1. Michelangelo: *Pietà; David; Madonna and Child;* ceiling of Sistine Chapel
2. Mies van der Rohe: Barcelona chair
3. Miró: *The Birth of the World*
4. Monet: water lily paintings
5. Munch: *The Scream*
6. Murillo: *Immaculate Conception*
7. O'Keeffe: *Cow's Skull*
8. Olmsted: Central Park
9. Picasso: *Three Musicians*
10. Pollock: *Autumn Rhythm*
11. Raphael: *Transfiguration*
12. Ray: "Tears"
13. Rembrandt: *Self Portrait with Sprouting Beard*
14. Remington: romantic scenes of the American Old West
15. Rockwell: *The Four Freedoms*
16. Rodin: *The Age of Bronze*
17. Rousseau: *The Dream*
18. Rubens: *The Elevation of the Cross*
19. Seurat: *Sunday Afternoon on the Island of La Grande Jatte*
20. Titian: *Assumption of the Virgin*
21. van Dyck: *Portrait of Charles I*
22. van Gogh: *Sunflowers*
23. Velázquez: *The Maids of Honor*

24. Warhol: *Ten Foot Flowers*
25. Whistler: *Whistler's Mother*
26. White: Washington Square Arch
27. Wood: *American Gothic*
28. Wren: St. Paul's Cathedral
29. Wright: Guggenheim Museum in New York City
30. Wyeth: *Ground Hog Day*

Words from Art: Dates and Types

BC

1. Greek: 900–30; harmony
2. Classical: 480–320; harmony
3. Hellenistic: 320–30; human movement
4. Roman: 509–395; harmony
5. Fayum Portrait: 400–1; portraiture on mummy

AD

6. Early Christian: 100–1453; mosaics
7. Byzantine: 527–1453; oriental motifs
8. Romanesque: 750–1400; rounded arches
9. Gothic: 1100–1400; elaborate architecture, stained-glass panels
10. Renaissance: 1350–1600 (da Vinci, Michelangelo, Raphael, Titian)
11. Mannerism: 1520s–1590s; distortion of human form (El Greco, Vassari)

12. Baroque: 1600–1700; grand theatrical effects (e.g., Palace of Versailles)

13. Rococo: 1730s–1780s; asymmetrical ornamentation, love of elegance

14. Neoclassicism: 1780–1820; restraint and balance

15. Romanticism: 1820–1840; imagination (Delacroix, Goya)

16. Realism: 1840–1865; the depressing with strict attention to details

17. Barbizon school: 1840–1870; landscape artists, portrayed nature as they saw it (Rousseau)

18. Modern art: 1850s–present; stresses form not matter

19. Impressionism: 1865–1905; visual impressions (Degas, Monet, Renoir)

20. Cubism: 1907–1915; geometrical forms (Braque, Picasso)

21. Surrealism: 1924–present; dreamlike images (Dalí, Magritte, Miró)

22. Expressionism: 1900s; stresses emotions (El Greco, Van Gogh)

23. Pop art: 1960–1965; art from popular culture (Warhol)

Words from Art: Dates and Types

1. Postimpressionism: 1900; pointillism (Seurat)

2. Pointillism: 1880s; dots of paint (Seurat)

3. Symbolism: 1885; art depicted through dreams and illusions

4. Modernism: 1911–1960; a divergence from the past in art

5. Postmodernism: 1960–present; complex forms

6. Abstract expressionism: 1940–1950; emphasis on paint (Pollock)

7. Art Deco: 1920–1930; geometric forms (e.g., Chrysler Building in New York City)

8. Ash Can school: early 1900s; squalid aspects of urban life

9. Bauhaus architecture: 1919–1933 in Germany; geometric style

10. Beaux-Arts style: 1890–1920; formal and classical techniques

11. Fauvism: 1898–1908; harsh colors and distortions (Matisse)

12. Futurism: 1910 in Italy; moving parts of machines

13. Minimal art: 1960–1965; characterized by restraint

14. Serial art: 1960–1965; repetition of an image (Warhol)

15. Constructivism: since 1920s; three-dimensional art (e.g., Calder's mobiles)

16. Expressionism: 1900s; emphasis on expression of artist (El Greco, Van Gogh)

17. Kinetic art: 1900s; art that moves through motorized parts

Words from Math

1. algebra: a mathematical system that solves arithmetical problems through the use of letters to stand for numbers

2. geometry: a mathematical system involving relationships of points, lines, planes, and solids

3. trigonometry: a mathematical system making calculations from the relations between the sides and angles of triangles

4. abscissa: x is the horizontal distance of a point from a vertical scale

5. ordinate: y is the vertical distance of a point from a horizontal scale

6. radius vector: v is the line segment from the origin to any point p

7. integers: whole numbers both positive and negative

8. prime number: a number divisible only by 1 and the number itself

9. ordinal number: a number defining a position in a series

10. acute angle: an angle less than 90 degrees

11. right angle: an angle of 90 degrees

12. obtuse angle: an angle between 90 and 180 degrees

13. complementary angles: angles that when measured together are 90 degrees

14. Cartesian grid: a graph made up of a horizontal x-axis and a vertical y-axis

15. origin: the point where the x and y axes meet on a Cartesian grid

16. quadrant: a section of a Cartesian grid

17. proportion: a relationship between two ratios

Words from Math

1. mode: the number in a set that occurs most often
2. standard deviation: a measure of the set's variation from its average
3. distance = rate × time

   d = rt

   Example: Traveling 50 miles an hour = 50 miles × 1 hour
4. triangle: a three-sided figure that contains three angles that add up to 180 degrees
5. equilateral triangle: a triangle with three sides equal in length
6. isosceles triangle: a triangle with two of three sides equal in length
7. right triangle: a triangle in which one of the angles is a right (90 degree) angle
8. hypotenuse: the longest side of a right triangle; the side opposite the 90 degree angle
9. perimeter of a triangle: the distance around the triangle

   p = a + b + c
10. area of a triangle: the base times the height divided by 2

    a = bh/2
11. Pythagorean Theorem: in a right triangle, the square of the length of the hypotenuse equals the sum of the squares of the length of the other two sides

    $c^2 = a^2 + b^2$

12. Pi (π): the ratio between the circumference of a circle and its diameter

   $\pi = 3.1416$

   $\pi = c/d = $ circumference/diameter

Words from Math

1. radius of a circle: any line that extends from the center of the circle to the edge of the circle

   $r = d/2 = $ diameter/2

2. diameter: the distance across a circle

   $d = 2r$

3. circumference: the distance around a circle

   $c = 2\pi r = \pi d$

4. area of a circle: π times the square of the radius

   $a = \pi r^2$

5. volume of a three-dimensional figure: length times width times height

   $v = lwh$

6. volume of a circular cylinder: the area of the circle times the height

   $v = \pi r^2 h$

7. diagonal: the distance between any two corners inside a three-dimensional figure

   $d^2 = a^2 + b^2 + c^2$

   $d = \sqrt{a^2 + b^2 + c^2}$

8. surface area of a rectangular box: the sum of the areas of all its sides

9. ratio: a relationship between two quadrants
10. quadrilateral: a four-sided figure such as a square, a rectangle, a parallelogram, a rhombus, and a trapezoid
11. volume: the amount of space a three-dimensional shape takes up
12. scalene triangle: a triangle with no equal sides and no equal angles
13. reciprocal: the inverse of a number

Words and Formulas from Math and Physics

1. probability: the likelihood of an event happening
   probability = x / total outcomes
2. permutation: an arrangement in a definite order
   permutation = x factorial
   Example: four factorial = 4! = 4 × 3 × 2 × 1 = 24
3. integer: a whole number, positive or negative, including zero
4. digits: the numbers 1 to 9
5. even number: an integer that can be divided evenly by 2
6. odd number: an integer that cannot be divided evenly by 2
7. prime number: a positive integer, excluding 0 and 1, divisible only by itself and the number 1
   Example: 2, 3, 5, 7
8. factor: a number x is a factor of y if y can be divided by x without leaving a remainder
9. product: the result of multiplication

10. quotient: the result of division

11. numerator: the top number of a fraction

12. denominator: the bottom number of a fraction

13. decimal: a fraction in a different form, using a decimal point

    Example: $0.5 = 5/10$

14. exponent: a number y multiplied by itself a specified number of times x

    Example: $2^3 = 2 \times 2 \times 2 = 8$

15. square root: y equals x squared or multiplied by itself $\sqrt{y} = x$, or $y = x^2$

    Example: $= \sqrt{16} = 4$

16. $=$: equal to

17. $\neq$: is not equal to

18. $>$: is greater than

19. $<$: is less than

20. $\geq$: is greater than or equal to

21. $\leq$: is less than or equal to

22. counting numbers: 1, 2, 3, 4, etc.

23. whole numbers: 0, 1, 2, 3, 4, etc.

24. integers: $-2, -1, 0, 1, 2$, etc.

25. percent: a way of expressing a fraction

    Example: $5/10 = 50\%$

26. average of a set of numbers: the sum or total value divided by the amount of numbers in the set

27. median: the middle value in a set of numbers

Words from Chemistry

1. chemistry: the study of the elements and the compounds they form and the reactions they undergo
2. elements: the basic building blocks of all other substances
3. periodic table: an arrangement of the chemical elements with their respective symbols, atomic numbers, and atomic weights
4. compound: a substance containing atoms of more than one element
5. mole: the amount of the substance equal in grams to the sum of the atomic weight
6. atoms: the smallest units of elements
7. ion: an electrically charged atom or group of atoms
8. radioactivity: the emission of subatomic particles from a nucleus
9. proton: a subatomic particle with a positive charge
10. electron: a subatomic particle with a negative charge
11. covalent bond: a bond of atoms linked together by sharing electrons
12. ionic bond: a bond of atoms linked together by the attraction of unlike charges
13. polar bond: a bond with both ionic and covalent characteristics
14. organic chemistry: an area of chemistry dealing with carbon compounds
15. states of matter: solid, liquid, and gas
16. acid: a compound that yields H^+ ions in solution

17. base: a compound that yields OH^- ions in solution
18. oxidation: a reaction with a loss of electrons
19. reduction: a reaction with a gain of electrons
20. electrochemical cell: a device that uses a chemical reaction to produce an electric current
21. equilibrium: a balanced condition resulting from opposing reactions
22. Le Chatelier's principle: a reasoning tool stating that if a system in equilibrium is disturbed, it adjusts so as to minimize the disturbance
23. thermodynamics: the study of energy
24. entropy: the thermodynamic quantity measuring the disorder of a substance
25. second law of thermodynamics: the total entropy of a chemical system always increases if the change is spontaneous

Words from Biology

1. biology: the study of living things
2. atom: the smallest part of an element that can take part in a chemical reaction
3. elements: the fundamental building blocks of all living things; more than one hundred exist
4. molecule: a precise arrangement of atoms
5. compound: a collection of molecules
6. acids: chemical compounds that release hydrogen ions when placed in water

7. bases: chemical compounds that attract hydrogen atoms when placed in water

8. organic compounds: the chemical compounds of living things

9. carbohydrates: molecules composed of carbon, hydrogen, and oxygen; the ratio of hydrogen atoms to oxygen atoms is 2:1

10. lipids: molecules composed of carbon, hydrogen, and oxygen; the ratio of hydrogen atoms to oxygen atoms is higher than in carbohydrates

11. proteins: compositions of amino acids that contain carbon, hydrogen, oxygen, and nitrogen atoms

12. nucleic acids: large molecules that contain a carbohydrate molecule, a phosphate group, and a nitrogenous base

13. prokaryotes: organisms such as bacteria that do not contain a nucleus or internal organelles

14. eukaryotes: organisms that contain a nucleus and internal organelles

15. cytoplasm: a semiliquid substance that contains organelles

16. organelles: microscopic bodies within the cytoplasm that perform distinct functions

17. ribosomes: organelle bodies bound to the endoplasmic reticulum that are the sites of protein synthesis

18. Golgi apparatus: an organelle that is the site of protein and lipid processing

19. enzymes: proteins that catalyze chemical reactions within cells

20. mitochondrion: the organelle that is the site of energy production within cells

Words from Biology

1. nucleus: the organelle that contains the genetic material DNA

2. diffusion: the movement of molecules from a region of higher concentration to one of lower concentration

3. osmosis: the diffusion involving only water molecules and often across a semipermeable membrane

4. adenosine triphosphate (ATP): the chemical that provides the energy in cells

5. active transport: the movement of molecules across a membrane from a region of lower concentration to a region of higher concentration; the energy needed is derived from ATP

6. photosynthesis: the process in plants of utilizing energy to synthesize carbohydrates

7. cellular respiration: the process in animals of obtaining energy from carbohydrates

8. glycolysis: the process in which one glucose molecule is broken down

9. Krebs cycle: the subdivision of cellular respiration in which pyruvic acid is broken down and the resulting energy is used to form high-energy compounds

10. chemosmosis: the production of ATP in cellular respiration

11. fermentation: an anaerobic process in which energy is released from glucose

12. mitosis: a type of cell division occurring in phases (pro-
    phase, metaphase, anaphase, and telophase) that results
    in two daughter cells each with the same number and
    kind of chromosomes as the parent cell; the process
    by which cells reproduce

13. meiosis: a type of cell division by which the chromo-
    some number is halved during gamete formation; the
    process by which sperm cells and egg cells are produced

14. zygote: a fertilized egg cell

15. genome: the set of all genes that specify an organism's
    traits

16. genotype: the gene composition of a living organism

17. phenotype: the expression of the genes of a living or-
    ganism

18. Gregor Mendel: the man who developed the science
    of genetics in the 1860s and 1870s

19. taxonomy: the science of classification of organisms

20. moneran: a kingdom that includes bacteria

21. protista: a kingdom that includes protozoa, algae, and
    slime molds

22. fungi: a kingdom that includes molds, mushrooms,
    mildews, and yeasts

23. invertebrates: animals with no backbones such as Po-
    rifera (sponges), Cnidaria (jellyfish), Platyhelminthes
    (tapeworms), Aschelminthes (roundworms), Annelida
    (earthworms), Mollusca (snails, squids, oysters, octo-
    puses), Arthropoda (spiders, ticks, lobsters, insects),
    Echinodermata (sea urchins), and some Chordata
    (reptiles)

24. vertebrates: animals with backbones, such as Osteichthyes (fish), Salientia and Gymnophiona (amphibians), some Chordata (reptiles), Ave (birds), and Mammalia (mammals)

Words from Neurology and Psychiatry

1. brain: the portion of the central nervous system that is located within the skull; the receiver, organizer, and distributor of information for the body. The brain has several parts: the cerebrum, limbic system, and basal ganglia; the diencephalon with the thalamus, hypothalamus, pituitary gland, and pineal gland; the midbrain; the pons and medulla; and the cerebellum. The brain weighs approximately three pounds, is composed of more than two hundred billion neurons, consists of right and left halves, and operates twenty-four hours a day. It directs all thinking, feeling, moving, talking, and activity, and makes us human.

2. afferent neuron: a neuron that carries an impulse toward the central nervous system

3. agonist: drugs that alter the physiology of a cell or neuron by binding to a receptor, producing an effect in the brain and therefore the body

4. amino acids: organic acids containing a carboxyl group (COOH) and an amino group (NH_2); the basic units from which proteins are formed

5. amygdala: the part of the brain's limbic system that has to do with memory and emotionally charged events

6. Asperger's syndrome: a mental disorder starting in childhood and characterized by impairment in social interaction

7. autistic thinking: thinking that is egocentric and often seen in schizophrenia

8. cytochrome P450 enzymes (P450): an enzyme system in the liver that metabolizes most psychiatric and other medical drugs; it is so named because it strongly absorbs light at a wavelength of 450 nanometers

9. delirium tremens (d.t.'s): a severe and sometimes fatal brain disorder that commonly occurs four to five days after cessation of heavy consumption of alcohol

10. ego alien: thoughts that are repugnant, recurrent, unwanted, undesired, and not consistent with a person's usual thinking; they occur in obsessive-compulsive anxiety disorder (OCD)

11. generic drug: a drug named by the U.S. Food and Drug Administration (FDA); the brand name is the name given by the pharmacy company

12. hallucination: false sensory perceptions that can be auditory, visual, or tactile

13. hypochondriasis: a mental disorder whereby one is preoccupied with fears of having a serious medical disease

14. hypothalamic/pituitary/adrenal axis (HPA): three structures (hypothalamus, pituitary gland, and adrenal gland) that form the basis of the fight-or-flight stress response

Words from Physics

1. $E = mc^2$: theory of relativity (E = energy, m = mass, c^2 = the speed of light squared)
2. physics: the science dealing with the interaction of matter and energy
3. thermodynamics: the science of the reversible transformation of heat into other forms of energy
4. entropy: disorder
5. joule: a unit of energy
6. Newtonian mechanics: a system of mechanics that relies on Newton's laws of motion
7. heat: energy arising from the random motion of the molecules of bodies
8. electricity: energy resulting from the existence of charged particles
9. magnetism: the study of the phenomena of being attracted by a magnet
10. light: a form of radiant energy
11. electromagnetism: magnetic forces produced by electricity
12. radioactivity: the spontaneous disintegration of atomic nuclei with the emission of particles
13. optics: the branch of physics dealing with light and vision
14. fission: a process in which the nucleus of an unstable atom splits into parts, releasing energy and neutrons
15. antimatter: a form of matter that has the same mass of an electron but with a positive charge

16. isotope: an atom of an element with a normal number of protons but a different number of neutrons in its nucleus

17. Manhattan Project: the project undertaken by the United States in World War II to build the first atomic bomb

18. cosmology: the study of the universe

19. second law of thermodynamics: all systems left to themselves decompose; systems go from order to disorder, not the reverse

14

Scripture Memorization and Neuroplasticity

Through faith we understand that the worlds were framed by the word of God, so that things which are seen were not made of things which do appear.

Hebrews 11:3 (KJV)

Do you have a favorite poem, piece of prose, or Bible verse? The above is one of mine.

Hebrews 11:3 is certainly interesting, as is the word *framed* in the verse. The word *frame* has at least twelve different meanings. In the above passage it denotes the following: "create," "devise," "fashion," "form," or "make."

It is exciting to think of the power involved here. God simply spoke his word and created the universe. That is truly recondite when one considers the enormous size of the universe. If you were to travel near the speed of light (approximately 186,000 miles per second) across the Milky Way alone, which is only one galaxy of many billions of galaxies, you would be 100,000 years old before completing the journey. This is almost unfathomable. If God's spoken word can create that, what can his written Word do for our brains?

Incidentally, I said *near* the speed of light, because at the speed of light, time would stand still—remember $E = mc^2$?

Select Bible Passages

We are, to a degree, what we repeatedly take into our brains. As we begin to expand our mental capacity through memorization, the brain chemistry is rearranged and memory is stored. Not only do we gain greater memory capability, but our brains actually change and improve. It is as if we program the brain with new software, and therefore we can respond to life around us in a healthier manner.

If what we take into our brains, then, ultimately defines us, what kinds of things do you want to put into your mind? How do you want to be defined? I believe that utilizing the Bible in memorization exercises can define you in a more positive way.

Here are some Bible verses worthy of memorization. They emphasize grace, mercy, forgiveness, encouragement, and help in times of need. I strongly suggest that the verses be written on three-by-five cards and that you always carry at least one card within easy reach; anytime you are prone to worry, you can immediately redirect your brain to the Bible verse and words of encouragement.

You may say, "But this is such a simple technique." I would respond by emphasizing the power of God's Word. Note the words of Christ in John 6:63: "The words that I speak to you are spirit, and they are life." And the words of the writer to the Hebrews: "For the word of God is living and powerful, and sharper than any two-edged sword, piercing even to the division of soul and spirit, and of joints and marrow, and is a discerner of the thoughts and intents of the heart" (4:12). And finally, the words of Luke: "And they said to one another, 'Did not our heart burn within us while He talked with us on the road, and while He opened the Scriptures to us?'" (24:32).

This simple but powerful behavioral technique also can carry divine strength for anyone. I personally began to memorize Scripture as a youth in my father's Sunday school class. Initially I memorized individual verses, then passages, and finally entire books of the Bible. It changed my life. It developed my ability to remember. It can do the same for you. The memorization of Scripture through the Holy Spirit's empowerment is the most important tool for spiritual growth I have ever implemented.

No force is a match for the Word of God. As effective as word memorization is, it pales in significance to memorizing and applying God's Word. If you want to develop a godly, brilliant mind, Scripture memorization is for you.

101 Bible Passages

The Scriptures quoted here for memorization are taken from the New King James Version of the Bible. However, you may choose to use your favorite version to memorize these passages.

1. Genesis 18:14: "Is anything too hard for the LORD?"

2. Deuteronomy 32:46–47: "And he said to them: 'Set your hearts on all the words which I testify among you today, which you shall command your children to be careful to observe—all the words of this law.

    "'For it is not a futile thing for you, because it is your life.'"

3. Joshua 1:8: "This Book of the Law shall not depart from your mouth, but you shall meditate in it day and night, that you may observe to do according to all that is written in it. For then you will make your way prosperous, and then you will have good success."

4. 1 Kings 19:4–8: "But he himself went a day's journey into the wilderness, and came and sat down under a broom tree. And he prayed that he might die, and said, 'It is enough! Now, LORD, take my life, for I am no better than my fathers!'

    "Then as he lay and slept under a broom tree, suddenly an angel touched him, and said to him, 'Arise and eat.' Then he looked, and there by his head was a cake baked on coals, and a jar of water. So he ate and drank, and lay down again. And the angel of the LORD came back the second time, and touched him, and said, 'Arise and eat, because the journey is too great for you.' So he arose, and ate and drank; and he went in the strength of that food forty days and forty nights as far as Horeb, the mountain of God."

5. 1 Chronicles 4:10: "And Jabez called on the God of Israel saying, 'Oh, that You would bless me indeed, and enlarge my territory, that Your hand would be with me,

and that You would keep me from evil, that I may not cause pain!' So God granted him what he requested."

6. 2 Chronicles 16:9: "For the eyes of the LORD run to and fro throughout the whole earth, to show Himself strong on behalf of those whose heart is loyal to Him."

7. Psalm 1:1–3: "Blessed is the man who walks not in the counsel of the ungodly, nor stands in the path of sinners, nor sits in the seat of the scornful; but his delight is in the law of the LORD, and in His law he meditates day and night. He shall be like a tree planted by the rivers of water, that brings forth its fruit in its season, whose leaf also shall not wither; and whatever he does shall prosper."

8. Psalm 18:16: "He sent from above, He took me; He drew me out of many waters."

9. Psalm 23:1–3: "The LORD is my shepherd; I shall not want. He makes me to lie down in green pastures; He leads me beside the still waters. He restores my soul."

10. Psalm 27:13–14: "I would have lost heart, unless I had believed that I would see the goodness of the LORD in the land of the living. Wait on the LORD; be of good courage, and He shall strengthen your heart; wait, I say, on the LORD!"

11. Psalm 34:4: "I sought the LORD, and He heard me, and delivered me from all my fears."

12. Psalm 37:23–24: "The steps of a good man are ordered by the LORD, and He delights in his way. Though he fall, he shall not be utterly cast down; for the LORD upholds him with His hand."

13. Psalm 40:2: "He also brought me up out of a horrible pit, out of the miry clay, and set my feet upon a rock, and established my steps."

14. Psalm 42:1: "As the deer pants for the water brooks, so pants my soul for You, O God."

15. Psalm 55:17: "Evening and morning and at noon I will pray, and cry aloud, and He shall hear my voice."

16. Psalm 56:3: "Whenever I am afraid, I will trust in You."

17. Psalm 57:1: "Be merciful to me, O God, be merciful to me! For my soul trusts in You; and in the shadow of Your wings I will make my refuge, until these calamities have passed by."

18. Psalm 73:25–26: "Whom have I in heaven but You? And there is none upon earth that I desire besides You.

    "My flesh and my heart fail; but God is the strength of my heart and my portion forever."

19. Psalm 91:15: "He shall call upon Me, and I will answer him; I will be with him in trouble; I will deliver him and honor him."

20. Psalm 103:12–14: "As far as the east is from the west, so far has He removed our transgressions from us. As a father pities his children, so the LORD pities those who fear Him. For He knows our frame; He remembers that we are dust."

21. Psalm 119:24: "Your testimonies also are my delight and my counselors."

22. Proverbs 21:31: "The horse is prepared for the day of battle, but deliverance is of the LORD."

23. Ecclesiastes 4:9–10: "Two are better than one, because they have a good reward for their labor. For if they fall, one will lift up his companion. But woe to him who is alone when he falls, for he has no one to help him up."

24. Isaiah 26:3: "You will keep him in perfect peace, whose mind is stayed on You, because he trusts in You."

25. Isaiah 40:8: "The grass withers, the flower fades, but the word of our God stands forever."

26. Isaiah 41:10: "Fear not, for I am with you; be not dismayed, for I am your God. I will strengthen you, yes, I will help you, I will uphold you with My righteous right hand."

27. Isaiah 43:2: "When you pass through the waters, I will be with you; and through the rivers, they shall not overflow you. When you walk through the fire, you shall not be burned, nor shall the flame scorch you."

28. Isaiah 43:18: "Do not remember the former things, nor consider the things of old."

29. Jeremiah 15:16: "Your words were found, and I ate them, and Your word was to me the joy and rejoicing of my heart; for I am called by Your name, O LORD God of hosts."

30. Jeremiah 29:11: "For I know the thoughts that I think toward you, says the LORD, thoughts of peace and not of evil, to give you a future and a hope."

31. Lamentations 3:22–23: "Through the LORD's mercies we are not consumed, because His compassions fail not. They are new every morning; great is Your faithfulness."

32. Nahum 1:7: "The LORD is good, a stronghold in the day of trouble; and He knows those who trust in Him."

33. Zechariah 4:6: "'Not by might nor by power, but by My Spirit,' says the LORD of hosts."

34. Matthew 6:34: "Therefore do not worry about tomorrow, for tomorrow will worry about its own things. Sufficient for the day is its own trouble."

35. Matthew 7:24–25: "Therefore whoever hears these sayings of Mine, and does them, I will liken him to a wise man who built his house on the rock: and the rain descended, the floods came, and the winds blew and beat on that house; and it did not fall, for it was founded on the rock."

36. Matthew 11:28–30: "Come to Me, all you who labor and are heavy laden, and I will give you rest. Take My yoke upon you and learn from Me, for I am gentle and lowly in heart, and you will find rest for your souls. For My yoke is easy and My burden is light."

37. Luke 18:1: "Then He spoke a parable to them, that men always ought to pray and not lose heart."

38. Luke 24:32: "And they said to one another, 'Did not our heart burn within us while He talked with us on the road, and while He opened the Scriptures to us?'"

39. John 1:12: "But as many as received Him, to them He gave the right to become children of God, to those who believe in His name."

40. John 3:16: "For God so loved the world that He gave His only begotten Son, that whoever believes in Him should not perish but have everlasting life."

41. John 6:63: "It is the Spirit who gives life; the flesh profits nothing. The words that I speak to you are spirit, and they are life."

42. John 14:27: "Peace I leave with you, My peace I give to you; not as the world gives do I give to you. Let not your heart be troubled, neither let it be afraid."

43. Acts 2:25–26: "For David says concerning Him: 'I foresaw the LORD always before my face, for He is at my right hand, that I may not be shaken. Therefore my heart rejoiced, and my tongue was glad; moreover my flesh also will rest in hope.'"

44. Acts 15:11: "But we believe that through the grace of the Lord Jesus Christ we shall be saved in the same manner as they."

45. Acts 16:31: "So they said, 'Believe on the Lord Jesus Christ, and you will be saved, you and your household.'"

46. Acts 20:32: "So now, brethren, I commend you to God and to the word of His grace, which is able to build you up and give you an inheritance among all those who are sanctified."

47. Acts 27:25: "Therefore take heart, men, for I believe God that it will be just as it was told me."

48. Romans 1:16–17: "For I am not ashamed of the gospel of Christ, for it is the power of God to salvation for everyone who believes, for the Jew first and also for the Greek. For in it the righteousness of God is revealed from faith to faith; as it is written, 'The just shall live by faith.'"

49. Romans 3:22: "Even the righteousness of God, through faith in Jesus Christ, to all and on all who believe. For there is no difference."

50. Romans 3:24: "Being justified freely by His grace through the redemption that is in Christ Jesus."

51. Romans 3:26: "To demonstrate at the present time His righteousness, that He might be just and the justifier of the one who has faith in Jesus."

52. Romans 3:28: "Therefore we conclude that a man is justified by faith apart from the deeds of the law."

53. Romans 5:1–2: "Therefore, having been justified by faith, we have peace with God through our Lord Jesus Christ, through whom also we have access by faith into this grace in which we stand, and rejoice in hope of the glory of God."

54. Romans 7:18: "For I know that in me (that is, in my flesh) nothing good dwells; for to will is present with me, but how to perform what is good I do not find."

55. Romans 8:2: "For the law of the Spirit of life in Christ Jesus has made me free from the law of sin and death."

56. Romans 8:15: "For you did not receive the spirit of bondage again to fear, but you received the Spirit of adoption by whom we cry out, 'Abba, Father.'"

57. Romans 8:28: "And we know that all things work together for good to those who love God, to those who are the called according to His purpose."

58. Romans 8:32: "He who did not spare His own Son, but delivered Him up for us all, how shall He not with Him also freely give us all things?"

59. Romans 12:2: "And do not be conformed to this world, but be transformed by the renewing of your mind, that you may prove what is that good and acceptable and perfect will of God."

60. 1 Corinthians 10:13: "No temptation has overtaken you except such as is common to man; but God is faithful, who will not allow you to be tempted beyond what you are able, but with the temptation will also make the way of escape, that you may be able to bear it."

61. 2 Corinthians 1:3–4: "Blessed be the God and Father of our Lord Jesus Christ, the Father of mercies and God of all comfort, who comforts us in all our tribulation, that we may be able to comfort those who are in any trouble, with the comfort with which we ourselves are comforted by God."

62. 2 Corinthians 4:8–9: "We are hard-pressed on every side, yet not crushed; we are perplexed, but not in despair; persecuted, but not forsaken; struck down, but not destroyed."

63. 2 Corinthians 7:6: "Nevertheless God, who comforts the downcast, comforted us by the coming of Titus."

64. 2 Corinthians 12:9: "And He said to me, 'My grace is sufficient for you, for My strength is made perfect in weakness.' Therefore most gladly I will rather boast in my infirmities, that the power of Christ may rest upon me."

65. Galatians 2:16: "Knowing that a man is not justified by the works of the law but by faith in Jesus Christ, even we have believed in Christ Jesus, that we might be justified by faith in Christ and not by the works of

the law; for by the works of the law no flesh shall be justified."

66. Galatians 2:20–21: "I have been crucified with Christ; it is no longer I who live, but Christ lives in me; and the life which I now live in the flesh I live by faith in the Son of God, who loved me and gave Himself for me. I do not set aside the grace of God; for if righteousness comes through the law, then Christ died in vain."

67. Galatians 3:2–11: "This only I want to learn from you: Did you receive the Spirit by the works of the law, or by the hearing of faith? Are you so foolish? Having begun in the Spirit, are you now being made perfect by the flesh? Have you suffered so many things in vain—if indeed it was in vain?

"Therefore He who supplies the Spirit to you and works miracles among you, does He do it by the works of the law, or by the hearing of faith?—just as Abraham 'believed God, and it was accounted to him for righteousness.' Therefore know that only those who are of faith are sons of Abraham. And the Scripture, foreseeing that God would justify the Gentiles by faith, preached the gospel to Abraham beforehand, saying, 'In you all the nations shall be blessed.' So then those who are of faith are blessed with believing Abraham.

"For as many as are of the works of the law are under the curse; for it is written, 'Cursed is everyone who does not continue in all things which are written in the book of the law, to do them.' But that no one is justified by the law in the sight of God is evident, for 'the just shall live by faith.'"

68. Galatians 3:14: "That the blessing of Abraham might come upon the Gentiles in Christ Jesus, that we might receive the promise of the Spirit through faith."

69. Galatians 3:22: "But the Scripture has confined all under sin, that the promise by faith in Jesus Christ might be given to those who believe."

70. Galatians 3:24: "Therefore the law was our tutor to bring us to Christ, that we might be justified by faith."

71. Galatians 3:26: "For you are all sons of God through faith in Christ Jesus."

72. Galatians 5:6: "For in Christ Jesus neither circumcision nor uncircumcision avails anything, but faith working through love."

73. Ephesians 1:19: "And what is the exceeding greatness of His power toward us who believe, according to the working of His mighty power."

74. Ephesians 2:8–9: "For by grace you have been saved through faith, and that not of yourselves; it is the gift of God, not of works, lest anyone should boast."

75. Ephesians 4:26: "'Be angry, and do not sin': do not let the sun go down on your wrath."

76. Ephesians 6:10–12: "Finally, my brethren, be strong in the Lord and in the power of His might. Put on the whole armor of God, that you may be able to stand against the wiles of the devil. For we do not wrestle against flesh and blood, but against principalities, against powers, against the rulers of the darkness of this age, against spiritual hosts of wickedness in the heavenly places."

77. Philippians 2:4: "Let each of you look out not only for his own interests, but also for the interests of others."

78. Philippians 3:9: "And be found in Him, not having my own righteousness, which is from the law, but that which is through faith in Christ, the righteousness which is from God by faith."

79. Philippians 3:13–14: "Brethren, I do not count myself to have apprehended; but one thing I do, forgetting those things which are behind and reaching forward to those things which are ahead, I press toward the goal for the prize of the upward call of God in Christ Jesus."

80. Philippians 4:6: "Be anxious for nothing, but in everything by prayer and supplication, with thanksgiving, let your requests be made known to God."

81. Philippians 4:8: "Finally, brethren, whatever things are true, whatever things are noble, whatever things are just, whatever things are pure, whatever things are lovely, whatever things are of good report, if there is any virtue and if there is anything praiseworthy—meditate on these things."

82. Philippians 4:13: "I can do all things through Christ who strengthens me."

83. 1 Thessalonians 2:13: "For this reason we also thank God without ceasing, because when you received the word of God which you heard from us, you welcomed it not as the word of men, but as it is in truth, the word of God, which also effectively works in you who believe."

84. 1 Timothy 1:16: "However, for this reason I obtained mercy, that in me first Jesus Christ might show all

longsuffering, as a pattern to those who are going to believe on Him for everlasting life."

85. 2 Timothy 3:15: "And that from childhood you have known the Holy Scriptures, which are able to make you wise for salvation through faith which is in Christ Jesus."

86. Hebrews 4:12: "For the word of God is living and powerful, and sharper than any two-edged sword, piercing even to the division of soul and spirit, and of joints and marrow, and is a discerner of the thoughts and intents of the heart."

87. Hebrews 4:15: "For we do not have a High Priest who cannot sympathize with our weaknesses, but was in all points tempted as we are, yet without sin."

88. Hebrews 10:24–25: "And let us consider one another in order to stir up love and good works, not forsaking the assembling of ourselves together, as is the manner of some, but exhorting one another, and so much the more as you see the Day approaching."

89. Hebrews 10:35–36: "Therefore do not cast away your confidence, which has great reward. For you have need of endurance, so that after you have done the will of God, you may receive the promise."

90. Hebrews 11:3: "By faith we understand that the worlds were framed by the word of God, so that the things which are seen were not made of things which are visible."

91. Hebrews 11:31: "By faith the harlot Rahab did not perish with those who did not believe, when she had received the spies with peace."

92. Hebrews 12:1–3: "Therefore we also, since we are surrounded by so great a cloud of witnesses, let us lay aside every weight, and the sin which so easily ensnares us, and let us run with endurance the race that is set before us, looking unto Jesus, the author and finisher of our faith, who for the joy that was set before Him endured the cross, despising the shame, and has sat down at the right hand of the throne of God.

    "For consider Him who endured such hostility from sinners against Himself, lest you become weary and discouraged in your souls."

93. Hebrews 13:5: "Let your conduct be without covetousness; be content with such things as you have. For He Himself has said, 'I will never leave you nor forsake you.'"

94. James 2:23: "And the Scripture was fulfilled which says, 'Abraham believed God, and it was accounted to him for righteousness.' And he was called the friend of God."

95. James 4:7: "Therefore submit to God. Resist the devil and he will flee from you."

96. James 5:17: "Elijah was a man with a nature like ours, and he prayed earnestly that it would not rain; and it did not rain on the land for three years and six months."

97. 1 Peter 1:21: "Who through Him believe in God, who raised Him from the dead and gave Him glory, so that your faith and hope are in God."

98. 1 Peter 2:11: "Beloved, I beg you as sojourners and pilgrims, abstain from fleshly lusts which war against the soul."

99. 1 Peter 5:7: "Casting all your care upon Him, for He cares for you."

100. 1 John 1:9: "If we confess our sins, He is faithful and just to forgive us our sins and to cleanse us from all unrighteousness."

101. 1 John 2:14: "I have written to you, fathers, because you have known Him who is from the beginning. I have written to you, young men, because you are strong, and the word of God abides in you, and you have overcome the wicked one."

15

Key Questions about Neurogenesis

> Though I speak with the tongues of men and of angels, and have not charity, I am become as sounding brass, or a tinkling cymbal.
>
> 1 Corinthians 13:1 (KJV)

Early Modern English was often inimitable, poetic, and beautiful, as the above New Testament verse so aptly illustrates. Conversely, this version of our language often contained words that are more difficult for us to understand today. When considering the verse above from "the love chapter" in the Bible, most people know that *cymbal* is a percussive musical instrument with a circular brass plate that makes a sharp ringing sound when hit. However, many people today may not know the meaning of the word *charity* as used in this verse.

Americans usually define *charity* as an organization to which they donate money for a special cause, or as an act of benevolence toward another person or group. Yet in this biblical context, *charity* is another word for "love." In the English of the King James Bible, we are cautioned that our best and kindest words are just noise if not emanating from a heart of love.

●●●

The Good and Bad of Natural Products and Increased Cognition

As we discuss *neurogenesis* (the development and growth of nervous tissue), we must examine the issue from all angles and ask a number of key questions.

1. What part will nutrition and natural products play in neurogenesis?

I anticipate extensive research in this area. People have long sought "the fountain of youth," and I doubt they will stop now. However, so far, no natural product has a great track record in producing neurogenesis. And in spite of the fact that some of my colleagues advocate mentally enhancing herbs, I suggest keeping a wary eye on such products. Various herbs or supplements are taken for either cognitive enhancement in healthy people or dementia in the elderly. Yet only one has been developed into a scientifically proven substance for treatment of symptoms of Alzheimer's disease. That drug is galantamine, which is marketed as the prescription drug Reminyl for Alzheimer's dementia. Galantamine is derived from daffodils.

Other natural products tried and endorsed by consumers but not scientifically confirmed include ginkgo biloba, vitamin E, L-carnitine, choline, lecithin, "smart drugs" (piracetam, aniracetam, pramiracetam), phosphatidylserine, ginseng, SAMe (S-Adenosylmethionine), DHEA (dehydroepiandrosterone), melatonin, huperzia serrata, omega-3 fatty acids, vitamin C, coenzyme Q10, and vitamin B complex. Currently no evidence widely supports any true mental benefit for the user of these products.

Also, I suggest avoiding 5-HTP (5-Hydroxytryptophan) and L-tryptophan, precursors of serotonin. While it is true that serotonin may play a role in neurogenesis, there is a huge leap in logic to move from a precursor of serotonin to actual neurogenesis. Studies and literature remain lacking in support for advocating the use of these precursors; in fact, some evidence indicates that they may actually present a danger to those who use them.

Of all the natural products, omega-3 fatty acids might offer a little benefit. They decrease cholesterol and triglycerides and so might help mitigate atherosclerosis, which decreases blood flow to vital brain cells. Omega-3 fatty acids also slow the induction of calcium into the brain cells, conceivably helping in mood stabilization and mental focus.

It is true that much of the brain is composed of fatty acids; that increased oxidation can occur in the brain over time; that theoretically oxidation could contribute to cognitive decline; and that theoretically antioxidants (vitamin E, vitamin C, glutathione, n-acetyl-cysteine, selenium, carotenoids, and flavonoids) might slow this decline a bit. However, such reasoning is fictitious because in the majority of research studies documenting major benefits in preventing cognitive decline, such benefits are simply not present with these products.

Theoretically it is true that if we could better preserve the energy production system in the nervous system, we might think sharper; it is true that coenzyme Q10 and lipoid acid are involved in energy production, and that acetyl-l-carnitine is involved in the formation of acetylcholine, which is the main neurotransmitter involved in memory. However, even with such reasoning, it is probably fallacious to conclude that these chemicals can make a person think faster; research is lacking.

Theoretically it is true that herbs may have a slight effect on improved mental functioning, and that they work in various ways to do this. For example, ginkgo biloba might decrease blood viscosity, increase vascular contraction, increase cerebral blood flow, and have beneficial effects on beta-amyloid proteins. However, the benefits seem mild, and serious side effects (spontaneous bleeding and death) are possible. Panax ginseng has been touted to improve cognitive functioning, but it can also cause insomnia, hypertension, diarrhea, cerebral arteritis, and Stevens-Johnson syndrome, which can cause a potentially lethal rash. Huperzine A (also called Chinese moss) might help in cognitive delay because it increases acetylcholine, but why take Chinese moss when a drug that has been studied for years, such as Aricept, does the same thing?

Vinpocetine has been reported to enhance memory. It is a synthetic derivative of apovincamine, a compound in the periwinkle plant. It is purported to enhance cerebral blood flow, stimulate cerebral metabolism, and improve microcirculation in the brain. While preliminary clinical research suggests vinpocetine might enhance memory in normal volunteers and might have a modest effect on cognitive impairment in dementia, few double-blind controlled clinical studies have been published. Because vinpocetine inhibits drug-induced platelet aggregation, it also might interact with anticoagulant/antiplatelet drugs such as aspirin, Plavix, NSAIDs (nonsteroidal anti-inflammatory drugs), and warfarin.

Bacopa has been touted in India for memory enhancement. However, these reports are anecdotal, and the user runs the risk of contaminants (lead, arsenic, and mercury).

Brahmi, also called gotu kola, is another herb from India reputed to improve memory. These reports are anecdotal; research is lacking.

Maca is an herb from Peru reputed to enhance memory. These reports are anecdotal; research is lacking.

Reishi is a mushroom from Asia reputed to improve memory. These reports are anecdotal; research is lacking. Reishi can induce itching, an upset stomach, and bloody stools. It can interact with anticoagulant/antiplatelet drugs and antihypertensive medications.

It is true that daffodils contain galantamine, which inhibits acetylcholine esterase. This results in increased acetylcholine, which plays a role in memory. But why eat daffodils when those with dementia can ask their doctor about Reminyl (purified galantamine from daffodils), a prescription medication?

For natural products, the answer may lie not in which ones to take but in what to avoid—cigarettes and alcohol. Both directly or indirectly destroy many brain cells.

2. What part will psychopharmacology play in neurogenesis?

It is true that if there is some atrophy in the hippocampus from post-traumatic stress disorder (PTSD), then an SSRI (selective serotonin reuptake inhibitor) such as Zoloft (sertraline) seems to produce neurogenesis in some people. However, an SSRI will not produce neurogenesis in healthy individuals. Also, while it is true that an acetylcholinesterase inhibitor such as Aricept (donepezil) or an NMDA (N-methyl-Dutch-aspartate) inhibitor such as Namenda (memantine) may slow the progression of Alzheimer's dementia, these drugs also do not produce neurogenesis in healthy individuals.

3. What part will mental exercises play in neurogenesis?

Given the current lack of supportive evidence for the use of most natural products often endorsed today as mental enhancers, I believe that the current best hope for producing neurogenesis—and a brilliant mind—seems to lie in mental exercises such as those described in this book. History validates this; brilliant minds throughout the centuries were often assiduous in practicing mental exercises. We know that "enriched conditions" with mental exercises seem to retard mental decline, but I suspect such would produce neurogenesis, as well as increase the number of synapses, in any brain. Einstein, for instance, had not only a large brain but also a profundity of synapses. In addition to historical examples, scientific experiments from monkeys to man seem to verify neurogenesis.

We normally lose thousands of brain cells daily beginning in our early thirties. We lose 1 to 2 percent of our neural cells each year, and the loss increases significantly after age forty-five as measured by neuropsychological testing; this is known as *age-related cognitive decline*. Today's consumers eagerly seek products to halt this decline. Yet I believe the best tool we have for mitigating this decline in healthy individuals is not natural products, not nutrition, not "smart drugs," not medication, but mental exercises.

My hope is that you will try these exercises yourself to increase your own mental capacity, and also that you will share this tool with those you know to help them improve not only their mental states—through neurogenesis—but also their everyday lives.

Conclusion

I n this book you have been exposed to a host of exercises to increase your IQ, to create a brilliant mind. As you begin to use these mental techniques and memory lists, remember the importance of the following:

1. We think in words. Concepts are communicated in words. Arguments are won or lost through words. Words are the tools of thought. Memory is largely stored in words. IQ is largely tested on the words one knows. Words can be learned.

2. Both brain synapses and brain cells can be increased. Words are tools to accomplish this. It is probable that memorizing words or Scripture increases one's brain synapses and cells. The brain has neuroplasticity—the ability to change in response to experience.

3. A brilliant mind is ours for the taking. Choosing to memorize vocabulary and Scripture can be a step toward brilliance.

Notes

Chapter 1: A Brilliant Mind

1. Marilyn vos Savant and Leonore Fleischer, *Brain Building: Exercising Yourself Smarter* (New York: Bantam Books, 1990), 46.

2. Wilfred Funk and Norman Lewis, *30 Days to a More Powerful Vocabulary* (New York: Pocket Books, 1970), 4.

3. Charles Harrington Elster, *Verbal Advantage*. Audiocassette.

Chapter 2: Neuroplasticity

1. *World Book Encyclopedia*, vol. 3, s.v. "Churchill, Winston."

Chapter 3: Memory Techniques

1. Claude W. Olney, *Where There's a Will There's an A* (Paoli, PA: Chesterbrook Educational Publishers, 1991), 10.

2. Ibid.

Bibliography

Alcamo, I. Edward, and Kelly Schweitzer. *CliffsQuickReview Biology*. New York: Wiley Publishing, 2001.

The American Heritage Dictionary of the English Language. 4th ed. New York: Houghton Mifflin, 2000.

Anderson, Stevens W., ed. *The Great American Bathroom Book*. Vol. 1. Salt Lake City: Compact Classics, 1991.

———. *The Great American Bathroom Book*. Vol. 2. Salt Lake City: Compact Classics, 1993.

———. *The Great American Bathroom Book*. Vol. 3. Salt Lake City: Compact Classics, 1994.

Andreasen, Nancy D., and Donald W. Black. *Introductory Textbook of Psychiatry*. 2nd ed. Washington DC: American Psychiatric Press, 1995.

Ayd, Frank J., Jr. "Expanding Clinical Indications and Treatment Strategies for Psychopharmacology in the New Millennium." *International Drug Therapy Newsletter* 35, no. 10 (October 2000): 73.

Bannister, Roger. *Brain's Clinical Neurology*. 5th ed. Oxford: Oxford University Press, 1978.

Barlow, David H., and V. Mark Duram. *Abnormal Psychology: An Integrative Approach.* 4th ed. Belmont, CA: Wadsworth, 2005.

Barron's Student's Concise Encyclopedia. New York: Barron's, 1988.

Benjamin, Ludy T., Jr., J. Roy Hopkins, and Jack R. Nation. *Psychology.* 3rd ed. New York: Macmillan, 1994.

Bergin, James D. *Medicine Recall.* Baltimore: Lippincott Williams & Wilkins, 1997.

Berkhof, Louis. *Systematic Theology.* Carlisle, PA: Banner of Truth Trust, 1958.

Berry, George R. *The Interlinear Greek-English New Testament with Lexicon and Synonyms.* Grand Rapids: Zondervan, 1976.

Braunwald, Eugene, Kurt J. Isselbacher, Jean D. Wilson, et al., eds. *Harrison's Principles of Internal Medicine: Companion Handbook.* 14th ed. New York: McGraw-Hill, 1998.

Bridgewater, William, and Seymour Kurtz, eds. *The Columbia Encyclopedia.* 3rd ed. New York: Columbia University Press, 1967.

Brown, Colin, ed. *The New International Dictionary of New Testament Theology.* Vols. 1–3. Grand Rapids: Zondervan, 1979.

Burchers, Sam, Max Burchers, and Bryan Burchers. *Vocabulary Cartoons II.* Punta Gorda, FL: New Monic Books, 2000.

Buzan, Tony. *Make the Most of Your Mind.* New York: Simon & Schuster, 1984.

Cacioppo, John T., and Gary G. Berntson, eds. *Essays in Social Neuroscience.* Cambridge, MA: MIT Press, 2004.

Calvert, Gemma, Charles Spence, and Barry E. Stein, eds. *The Handbook of Multisensory Processes.* Cambridge, MA: MIT Press, 2004.

Carlson, Neil R. *Physiology of Behavior.* 8th ed. Boston: Pearson Educational, 2004.

———. *Psychology: The Science of Behavior.* Boston: Allyn & Bacon, 1990.

Chafer, Lewis Sperry. *Major Bible Themes*. Grand Rapids: Zondervan, 1974.

———. *Systematic Theology*. Vols. 1–8. Dallas: Dallas Seminary Press, 1948.

Charney, Dennis S., Eric J. Nestler, and Benjamin S. Bunny, eds. *Neurobiology of Mental Illness*. Oxford: Oxford University Press, 1999.

Clark, Ronald G. Manter and Gatz's *Essentials of Clinical Neuroanatomy and Neurophysiology*. 5th ed. Philadelphia: F. A. Davis, 1975.

Conn, P. Michael, ed. *Neuroscience in Medicine*. 2nd ed. Totowa, NJ: Humana Press, 2003.

Coyle, J. "Seeing a Placebo Work in the Brain." *Journal Watch Psychiatry* 7, no. 11 (November 2001): 85–86.

Dorland's Illustrated Medical Dictionary. 30th ed. Philadelphia: W. B. Saunders, 2003.

Douglas, J. D., ed. *The New Bible Dictionary*. Grand Rapids: Eerdmans, 1962.

Dox, Ida G., B. John Melloni, Gilbert M. Eisner, and June L. Melloni. *Melloni's Illustrated Medical Dictionary*. 4th ed. New York: Parthenon, 2002.

Dragonski, Bogdan. "Neuroplasticity: Changes in Gray Matter Induced by Training." *Nature*, no. 427 (January 2004): 311–12.

E.encyclopedia. London: Dorling Kindersley Limited, 2003.

Ellicott, Charles John. *Ellicott's Bible Commentary in One Volume*. Grand Rapids: Zondervan, 1971.

———, ed. *Ellicott's Commentary on the Whole Bible*. Grand Rapids: Zondervan, 1981.

Erickson, Millard J. *Christian Theology*. 2nd ed. Grand Rapids: Baker, 1998.

Fadem, Barbara, and Steven Simring. *Psychiatry Recall*. Baltimore: Lippincott Williams & Wilkins, 1997.

Feldman, Robert S. *Essentials of Understanding Psychology*. New York: McGraw-Hill, 1989.

Feltman, John, ed. *Prevention's Giant Book of Health Facts*. Emmaus, PA: Rodale Press, 1991.

Forster, Francis M. *Clinical Neurology*. 3rd ed. St. Louis: The C. V. Mosby Company, 1973.

Freedman, Alfred M., and Harold I. Kaplan. *The Child—His Psychological and Cultural Development*. New York: Atheneum, 1972.

Gaebelein, Frank E., ed. *The Expositor's Bible Commentary*. Grand Rapids: Zondervan, 1981.

Gelb, Douglas J. *Introduction to Clinical Neurology*. Philadelphia: Elsevier, 2005.

Geller, Barbara. "Juggling with a New Concept in Brain Plasticity." *Journal Watch Psychiatry* 10, no. 4 (April 2004): 1.

Gilroy, John. *Basic Neurology*. 3rd ed. New York: McGraw-Hill, 2000.

Goetz, Christopher G., ed. *Textbook of Clinical Neurology*. 2nd ed. Philadelphia: W. B. Saunders, 2003.

Goodrick, Edward W., and John R. Kohlenberger III. *Zondervan NIV Exhaustive Concordance*. 2nd ed. Grand Rapids: Zondervan, 1999.

Grinspoon, Lester, ed. "What Is a Nocebo?" *The Harvard Mental Health Letter* 14, no. 1 (July 1997): 8.

Grudem, Wayne. *Systematic Theology*. Grand Rapids: Zondervan, 1994.

Hall, John Whitney, and John Grayson Kirk, eds. *History of the World: Earliest Times to the Present Day*. North Dighton, MA: JG Press, 2002.

Handford, S. A., and Mary Herberg. *Langenscheidt's Pocket Latin Dictionary*. Berlin: Langenscheidt KG, 1966.

Harkavy, Michael D., ed. *The American Spectrum Encyclopedia: The New Illustrated Home Reference Guide.* New York: American Booksellers Association, 1991.

————. *The New Webster's International Encyclopedia.* Naples, FL: Trident Press International, 1999.

Harrison, R. K. *Leviticus: An Introduction and Commentary.* Downers Grove, IL: InterVarsity Press, 1980.

Henry, Matthew, and Thomas Scott. *Commentary on the Holy Bible.* Nashville: Thomas Nelson, 1979.

Hirsch, E. D., Jr., Joseph F. Kett, and James Trefil. *The New Dictionary of Cultural Literacy.* 3rd ed. Boston: Houghton Mifflin, 2002.

Jones, H. Royden, ed. *Netter's Neurology.* Teterboro, NJ: Icon Learning Systems, 2004.

Kaplan, Harold I., and Benjamin J. Sadock. *Comprehensive Textbook of Psychiatry.* 7th ed. Vols. 1 and 2. Baltimore: Lippincott Williams & Wilkins, 2000.

Kaufman, David Myland. *Clinical Neurology for Psychiatrists.* 3rd ed. Philadelphia: W. B. Saunders, 1990.

Keck, Paul, and Susan McElroy. *Overview of CNS Disorders 2001.* New York: McMahon, 2000.

Kipfer, Barbara Ann. *Roget's International Thesaurus.* 6th ed. New York: HarperResource, 2001.

Klamen, Debra L., and Philip Pan. *Psychiatry: PreTest Self-Assessment and Review,* 10th ed. New York: McGraw-Hill, 2004.

Kleinmuntz, Benjamin. *Essentials of Abnormal Psychology.* New York: Harper & Row, 1974.

Leonard, Brian E. *Fundamentals of Psychopharmacology.* 2nd ed. Chichester, England: Wiley Publishing, 1997.

Lerner, Marcia. *Cracking the Miller Analogies Test.* 3rd ed. New York: Random House, 2002.

Lewis, Norman. *Word Power Made Easy: The Complete Handbook for Building a Superior Vocabulary*. New York: Pocket Books, 1978.

Lezak, Muriel Deutsch. *Neuropsychological Assessment*. 3rd ed. Oxford: Oxford University Press, 1995.

Little, Paul E. *Know What You Believe*. Wheaton: Scripture Press, 1970.

Lorayne, Harry. *Super Memory, Super Student: How to Raise Your Grades in 30 Days*. Boston: Little, Brown, 1990.

Lullmann, Heinz, Klaus Mohr, Albrecht Ziegler, and Detlef Bieger. *Color Atlas of Pharmacology*. New York: Thieme Medical Publishers, 1993.

MacDonald, William. *Believer's Bible Commentary*. Nashville: Thomas Nelson, 1990.

Marieb, Elaine N. *Human Anatomy and Physiology*. 2nd ed. Redwood City, CA: Benjamin Cummings, 1992.

McCutcheon, Marc. *Roget's Superthesaurus*. 3rd ed. Cincinnati: Writer's Digest, 2003.

McNeil, Elton B., and Zick Rubin. *The Psychology of Being Human*. San Francisco: Canfield Press, 1977.

Medical Terminology: An Illustrated Guide. 4th ed. Baltimore: Lippincott Williams & Wilkins, 2004.

Memory Notebook of Nursing. 2nd ed. Vol. II. Waxahachie, TX: Gingerbread Press, 2003.

Memory Notebook of Nursing: Pharmacology and Diagnosis. Waxahachie, TX: Gingerbread Press, 2005.

Merriam-Webster's Collegiate Encyclopedia. Springfield, MA: Merriam-Webster, 2000.

Merriam-Webster's Medical Desk Dictionary. Rev. ed. Springfield, MA: Merriam-Webster, 2005.

The Merriam-Webster Thesaurus. Springfield, MA: Merriam-Webster, 2005.

Miller, James, and Nathan Fountain. *Neurology Recall*. Baltimore: Lippincott Williams & Wilkins, 1997.

Minirth, Frank. *In Pursuit of Happiness: Choices That Can Change Your Life*. Grand Rapids: Revell, 2004.

———. *The Minirth Guide for Christian Counselors*. Nashville: Broadman & Holman, 2003.

Minirth, Frank B., and Paul D. Meier. *Happiness Is a Choice: A Manual on the Symptoms, Causes, and Cures of Depression*. Grand Rapids: Baker, 1978.

Mitchell, James, and Jess Stein, eds. *The Random House Encyclopedia*. New York: Random House, 1990.

Morgan, Clifford T., Richard A. King, John R. Weisz, and John Schopler. *Introduction to Psychology*. 7th ed. New York: McGraw-Hill, 1986.

Mosby's Medical Dictionary. 6th ed. St. Louis: Mosby, 2002.

Nathan, Harold D., and Charles Henrickson. *CliffsQuickReview Chemistry*. New York: Wiley Publishing, 2001.

Neufeldt, Victoria, and Andrew N. Sparks, eds. *Webster's New World Dictionary*. Compact School and Office Edition. New York: Webster's New World, 1989.

The Neuropsychology of Memory Power, The Bornstein Memory Training System: How to Remember Facts, Figures, Names and Faces. Adapted from Arthur Bornstein, *Memory: Arthur Bornstein's Training Course*. Pleasanton, CA: SyberVisionSystems, 1989.

The New York Public Library Desk Reference. 3rd ed. New York: Macmillan, 1998.

Nicholl, W. Robertson, ed. *The Expositor's Greek Testament*. Vols. I–V. Grand Rapids: Eerdmans, 1980.

Nolte, John. *The Human Brain: An Introduction to Its Functional Anatomy*. 5th ed. St. Louis: Mosby, 2002.

Norback, Craig, and Peter Norback. *The Must Words: The 6000 Most Important Words for a Successful and Profitable Vocabulary.* New York: McGraw-Hill, 1979.

O'Brien, Patrick K. *Atlas of World History.* Concise ed. New York: Oxford University Press, 2002.

Ornstein, Robert, and Richard F. Thompson. *The Amazing Brain.* Boston: Houghton Mifflin, 1984.

The Oxford American Dictionary and Thesaurus with Language Guide. New York: Oxford University Press, 2003.

The Oxford American Dictionary of Current English. New York: Oxford University Press, 1999.

Pack, Phillip E. *CliffsQuickReview Anatomy and Physiology.* New York: Wiley Publishing, 2001.

Paxinos, George, and Jürgen K. Mai, eds. *The Human Nervous System.* 2nd ed. Boston: Elsevier Academic Press, 2004.

Ramachandran, Anand. *Pharmacology Recall.* Baltimore: Lippincott Williams & Wilkins, 2000.

Restak, Richard M. *The Brain.* Toronto: Bantam Books, 1984.

———. *The Modular Brain.* New York: Charles Scribner's Sons, 1994.

———. *The Secret Life of the Brain.* Washington DC: Joseph Henry Press, 2001.

Rodale, J. I., ed. *The Synonym Finder.* Completely revised by Laurence Urdang and Nancy LaRoche, eds. Emmaus, PA: Rodale Press, 1978.

Roget's 21st Century Thesaurus in Dictionary Form. 3rd ed. New York: Bantam Dell, 2005.

Ropper, Allan H., and Robert H. Brown. *Adams and Victor's Principles of Neurology.* 8th ed. New York: McGraw-Hill Professional, 2005.

Ryrie, Charles C. *Biblical Theology of the New Testament*. Chicago: Moody, 1959.

———. *So Great Salvation*. Wheaton: Victor, 1989.

———. *A Survey of Bible Doctrine*. Chicago: Moody, 1972.

Ryrie, Charles Caldwell, ed. *The Ryrie Study Bible, King James Version*. Chicago: Moody Press, 1978.

———. *The Ryrie Study Bible, New American Standard Version*. Chicago: Moody Press, 1976.

Sadock, Benjamin J., and Virginia A. Sadock, eds. *Kaplan & Sadock's Comprehensive Textbook of Psychiatry*. 8th ed. Vol. 1. Philadelphia: Lippincott Williams & Wilkins, 2005.

———. *Kaplan & Sadock's Comprehensive Textbook of Psychiatry*. 8th ed. Vol. 2. Philadelphia: Lippincott Williams & Wilkins, 2005.

———. *Kaplan & Sadock's Pocket Handbook of Clinical Psychiatry*. 4th ed. Philadelphia: Lippincott Williams & Wilkins, 2005.

Sadock, Benjamin J., Virginia A. Sadock, and Norman Sussman, eds. *Kaplan & Sadock's Pocket Handbook of Psychiatric Drug Treatment*. 4th ed. Philadelphia: Lippincott Williams & Wilkins, 2006.

Sahelian, Ray. *Bottom Line's Mind Boosting Secrets: Natural Supplements That Enhance Your Mind, Memory, and Mood*. Stamford, CT: Bottom Line Books, 2004.

Schumaker, David, ed. *Seven Language Dictionary*. New York: Gramercy Books, 1978.

Scofield, C. I., ed. *The New Scofield Study Bible*. Nashville: Thomas Nelson, 1982.

The Shorter Oxford English Dictionary. 5th ed. Vols. 1 and 2. New York: Oxford University Press, 2002.

Simpson, John F., and Kenneth R. Magee. *Clinical Evaluation of the Nervous System*. Boston: Little, Brown, 1973.

Smith, Jerome H., ed. *The New Treasury of Scripture Knowledge.* Nashville: Thomas Nelson, 1992.

Squire, Larry R. *Memory and Brain.* New York: Oxford University Press, 1987.

Stahl, Stephen M. *Essential Psychopharmacology: Neuroscientific Basis and Practical Applications.* 2nd ed. Cambridge: Cambridge University Press, 2000.

Stedman's Medical Dictionary. 27th ed. Baltimore: Lippincott Williams & Wilkins, 2000.

Stern, Theodore A., and John B. Herman, eds. *Massachusetts General Hospital Psychiatry Update and Board Preparation.* 2nd ed. New York: McGraw-Hill, 2004.

Sternberg, Robert J. *Barron's How to Prepare for the MAT: Miller Analogies Test.* 8th ed. Hauppauge, NY: Barron's Educational Series, 2001.

Thompson, Della, ed. *The Oxford Dictionary of Current English.* 2nd ed. Oxford: Oxford University Press, 1992.

Tierney, Lawrence M., Jr., Stephen J. McPhee, and Maxine A. Papadakis. *Current Medical Diagnosis & Treatment 2006.* 45th ed. New York: McGraw-Hill, 2006.

Tortora, Gerard J., and Sandra Reynolds Grabowski. *Principles of Anatomy and Physiology.* 8th ed. New York: HarperCollins, 1996.

Unger, Merrill F. *Unger's Bible Handbook.* Chicago: Moody, 1967.

Venolia, Jan. *The Right Word! How to Say What You Really Mean.* Berkeley, CA: Ten Speed Press, 2003.

Vine, W. E. *An Expository Dictionary of New Testament Words.* Old Tappan, NJ: Revell, 1966.

Vine, W. E., Merrill F. Unger, and William White Jr. *Vine's Complete Expository Dictionary of Old and New Testament Words.* Nashville: Thomas Nelson, 1985.

Vos Savant, Marilyn, and Leonore Fleischer. *Brain Building: Exercising Yourself Smarter*. New York: Bantam Books, 1990.

Walvoord, John F., and Roy B. Zuck. *The Bible Knowledge Commentary: New Testament Edition*. Wheaton: Victor Books, 1983.

Webster's Dictionary of Word Origins. Springfield, MA: Merriam-Webster, 1991.

Webster's New Universal Unabridged Dictionary. New York: Random House, 1996.

Webster's New World Roget's A–Z Thesaurus. Cleveland: Wiley Publishing, 1999.

Webster's Universal Dictionary and Thesaurus. Montreal: Tormont Publications, 1993.

Weiner, Howard L., and Lawrence P. Levitt. *Neurology*. 5th ed. Baltimore: Lippincott Williams & Wilkins, 1994.

Wilson, Jean D., et al., eds. *Harrison's Principles of Internal Medicine*. 12th ed. New York: McGraw-Hill, 1991.

Wood, Clement, ed. *The Complete Rhyming Dictionary Revised: Including the Poet's Craft Book*. Revised by Ronald J. Bogus. New York: Doubleday, 1991.

The World Book Atlas. Chicago: World Book, 1986.

Wortman, Camille, and Elizabeth F. Loftus. *Psychology*. New York: McGraw-Hill, 1992.

Youngblood, Ronald F., ed. *Nelson's New Illustrated Bible Dictionary*. Nashville: Thomas Nelson, 1995.

Yudofsky, Stuart C., and Robert E. Hales. *The American Psychiatric Press Textbook of Neuropsychiatry*. 3rd ed. Washington DC: American Psychiatric Association, 1997.

Zahler, Kathy A. *McGraw-Hill's MAT: Miller Analogies Test*. New York: McGraw-Hill, 2006.

Frank Minirth, MD (1946–2015) was president of the Minirth Clinic in Richardson, Texas, and an adjunct professor at Dallas Theological Seminary. He was the author or coauthor of several books, including the bestselling *Happiness Is a Choice* and *Strong Memory, Sharp Mind*.

PROVEN TECHNIQUES FOR
**IMPROVING AND
PROTECTING YOUR**
MEMORY

STRONG
MEMORY

ANTI-AGING STRATEGIES
FOR YOUR BRAIN

SHARP
MIND

FRANK MINIRTH, MD